AF093577

# THE MANY PIECES OF ME
### By Nancy Robles

Paperclip Publishing

THE MANY PIECES OF ME

Copyright © 2023 by Nancy Robles

Published by: Paperclip Publishing LLC

All rights reserved. This book or any portion thereof may not be reproduced or used in any manner whatsoever without the express written permission of the publisher, except for brief and direct quotations in a book review.

Some names and identifying details have been changed
to protect the privacy of individuals.

Editor: Noelle S. LeBlanc
Cover/Graphics: Vincent Murace
Typography: Diane M. Serpa

Library of Congress Control Number: 2023946225

ISBN: 979-8-9891077-0-4 (hard cover)

ISBN: 979-8-9891077-2-8 (paperback)

ISBN: 979-8-9891077-1-1 (eBook)

Printed by IngramSpark.com in the United States of America

First Printing: February 1, 2024

Paperclip Publishing LLC
3800 W Ray Road Suite #5,
Chandler, AZ 85226

www.paperclippublishing.com

*I dedicate this book to my children who gave me purpose when I had none. They gave me air when I couldn't breathe and gave me hope at my darkest moments. Today, they continue to be my anchor.*

*Also, thank you to all those who saw and heard me when I couldn't see myself—all those who have been my friend, mentor, advocate, and ride or die.*

*Finally, to all those who have and continue to struggle with mental health, trauma, and generational trauma. Keep fighting to heal; you are worth all the love and compassion.*

# Chapter 1 - The Journey to Recovery

We have pain that lies hidden so deep in our hearts that we often don't know it exists. It is pain that wreaks havoc on our minds and bodies. It sends our hearts on a constant search for more than they can handle in an effort to make it disappear. My journey to recovery started when my daughter Karinna said, "You need help. You should go to therapy"—and I reluctantly agreed. It was then that I embarked on a search for understanding that would open wounds that were more painful than any flesh wound I could ever experience. However, that same journey would bring me to my promised land. A place I'd yearned for my entire life—a place of safety and self-love.

I arrived at work, as usual, feeling anxious with a sense of emotional exhaustion almost as if I couldn't quite catch my breath—a feeling I was way too familiar with. It was common for me to find myself in this place where breathing took a great deal of effort, but I did it with a lack of sensation. I often found myself on autopilot, walking through a difficult world, usually thinking of the next thing that needed to be done or the next big accomplishment. It was exhausting, but the exhilaration I felt as I reached each goal almost fulfilled my constant search for something—for a love I'd not yet experienced. A love that a girl receives only from a father figure who gives unconditional acceptance. A love that teaches her how to accept love and be loved in the future.

On this particular day, after my five-a.m. workout and ninety-minute drive to work that consisted of multiple calls from home regarding one or several of my five kids, I decided that I was reaching my breaking point. I'd tiptoed around it so many times in the past that it was a familiar place. It was a place where I couldn't tell what my body was doing, and my mind was having trouble using its old tricks to escape the pain of my past and present. I went for a walk during my lunch break and called the seven therapists I'd found earlier that day—all of whom practiced within walking distance of my office. I left desperate messages summarizing eight years of physical abuse and a lifetime of pain in only thirty seconds. The response I received changed my life.

Sandi, the only person who called me back, would go on to become a compass in my life. I made an appointment, and just days later, I met her for the first time. Sandi was younger than me, looked slightly ethnic, and had a very kind and gentle voice. She sat and listened to me recite years of abuse, neglect, trauma, and pain over forty-five minutes. She kindly cued me through the session and mostly just listened. It was like recalling a movie I'd watched, not my own life. The level of disassociation I had cultivated was necessary for my survival—and it's also what enabled my abusers, past and present, to keep me trapped.

In the first few sessions, we primarily discussed the reasons why I wanted to get divorced and how my husband, Kevin, had hurt me over the years. I'd go on angry and desperate rants about his constant unhappiness with me and the resentment I felt. Still, I realize now, I often minimized the reality. I took responsibility for my contribution to the argument and happily focused on how I could change my actions, giving me a false sense of control. I believed if I could control my behavior, then I could change the outcome of the story.

In those early sessions, we spent a lot of time discussing my need for control, which I mistakenly understood to mean that I was the problem. I angered my husband because I was controlling. It gave me a false sense of responsibility for his poor behavior. In fact, I made myself responsible for the behavior of every member of my family; their mistakes were my mistakes. Their mistakes were also accompanied by my shame and guilt—shame for not being a better parent and guilt for not being a good enough parent. It was a vicious cycle of self-hatred.

We discussed at length how Kevin had hurt my children. I talked about the constant feeling of walking on eggshells and his incessant unhappiness. How could I work so hard to make this man love me but still he responds with disdain? It would be years before I would understand the many ways my husband abused me beyond the physical attacks on my body. The slow, insidious damage to my mind and nervous system was by far much more difficult to recognize but equally as damaging. I didn't even know it was happening.

Weeks turned into months, and life was flying by. As the mother of five kids with a career in full swing and a constant need to prove my worth, every day was a full day. My three older children were young people navigating an unstable household and a world they were not prepared for. My oldest daughter, now in college, struggled with anxiety and a newly diagnosed eating disorder. She had pain in her heart that stemmed back to her birth into an incredibly unstable home resulting from the sadistic abuser who was her father and my first husband. This man was cruel for pleasure. He enjoyed the pain of others like a drug. He experienced the ultimate adrenaline rush from watching others suffer in the worst ways.

Bryanna, my younger daughter, was in a state of instability. She'd left home just months before after she'd reached her breaking point. She'd had enough of the home where she was not allowed to have an opinion or challenge her stepfather in the simplest ways. A house where a mistake would cause you to become invisible, almost nonexistent. Bryanna knew first-hand that it was everyone for themselves because her stepfather's approval and love depended on it.

Sebastian, my eldest son and last child from my first marriage, was in high school struggling with a heavy heart. A heart that was full of words that pierced through his mind in an endless loop. The words made him feel not seen or heard—followed by words of disappointment, dishonor, and disrespect more often than tolerable. Sebastian played and replayed moments attempting to figure out how he could recreate the ones that gave him hope of the love he so desired while also replaying the many occasions where his mistakes were meticulously elevated to a level of ultimate disloyalty.

Kyle, at just seven years old, was figuring out how to navigate a world that was not created for him. Although not fully aware of the expectations imposed by the society around him, he had to assimilate. He was focused on developing the necessary skills used to read social queues and societal norms. All I could see was my perfect and beautiful child struggling to fit in. Kyle had his father's approval but never quite his attention.

And then there was Dylan, a spunky three-year-old that I knew would push boundaries—even the boundaries set by his cruel father. He was a handful, needing more parental love from his father and constantly demanding from me physically and emotionally. Life often felt exhausting and all-consuming, as though it could drown me at any moment. It was the ultimate circus performance, a fragile balancing act that was always tilted to fit my husband's narrative, the coping mechanism of a fragile man.

The days were filled with emergencies, crises, disappointments, and fears, and somewhere in between, I had to fit in love for everyone…I constantly lost myself. Then add a pressure-filled career that demanded perfection at every step and shone a spotlight on any failures. I was in a constant state of hypervigilance and anxiety to the point where I didn't know the difference between fear, anxiety, and excitement. It all ran together like a brook that runs between boulders and carries more than water through its current.

Eventually, the therapy sessions started to focus on my past, far back into my childhood. It is an interesting experience to open up the memory box of our childhood. To purposely recount the memories we work so hard to discard is painful and liberating all at once. It was hard at times because the session would get hijacked by current events like the kids' fights or my husband's subtle tactics of abuse. Still, we persisted and kept going back to that scary place I'd worked so hard to leave behind. This place was full of unknowns because I didn't know what I would find. I'd created my own narrative that worked for so long.

In my story, my father loved me like no other and he would fill my heart with joy every time I heard his voice or saw his face. In my story, he loved me above all and was heartbroken to lose me. His love was undeniable, and we'd spent endless hours together. In my story, my dad was my hero, and it was only in the author's notes that a small notation existed regarding his serial cheating, the physical abuse he imposed on my mother and siblings, and his alcoholism. The story was soaked in this unconditional and platonic love my father felt for me, like no other I ever experienced. It was the love that would have grounded me and helped me love myself.

I would go on to explore my mother's love and her inability to live up to the task of motherhood. She tried but didn't have the tools she needed to provide basic protection or guidance for my siblings and me. I recall mechanically recounting sexual abuse dating back to the age of five. I'd repeated the stories before to other therapists, friends, or even partners. It was always like recounting an event I watched in a movie that wasn't real and didn't evoke complete despair. I recounted the neighbor's first violation, my stepfather's violations, the teacher's violation, and even the violations committed by random strangers and abusers disguised as lovers. As I detailed these events, it seemed unreal and far too much to bear. I couldn't possibly give myself the space to feel the loss each of these events provoked in me, it would be an all-consuming darkness that would drown me. Sandi knew that we had to open the door slowly to allow me to survive and let the sunshine in my heart again. I was so deeply afraid to open up the memory box which held these memories yet I desperately wanted to find peace and just live. I needed to stop running from the pain by filling my life with too much noise.

Our sessions became filled with tears and stories that made up the sad existence of a little girl who was me. I began to embody tremendous pain that became part of my very soul. I recall the session when I discussed the first time a man violated my body and stole a small part of me. I explained to Sandi how we lived in Costa Rica during this time and my parents were still together although their marriage was extremely unstable. I'd already witnessed my father physically assaulting my mother on more than one occasion. We were a middle-class family and lived in what was considered a pretty nice house. We had tile floor throughout the house, a front yard and a washing machine which was a hot commodity at the time. Our home had three bedrooms and the living room had a section for my mother to cut hair as she was a stay home mom but had received formal training in cosmetology. The backyard, once an immense piece of empty land, was now occupied by a full house with a family. These renters became my parent's friends, primarily my mother's friends as she was the stay home parent. Actually most moms were stay-at-home moms in the '70s. The family consisted of a mom, several kids, a husband and the mom's brother. The mom's brother was extremely friendly with my mom, so much so, that my parents fought over him on a few occasions. I recalled a warm sunny day on their porch, I sat on his lap because he was going to show me how to play the guitar. I was five and he was an adult, I'd guess in his 30's. He initially played a little while I sat on his lap and then proceeded to show me how to play. He placed my hands on the guitar and while my little fingers fumbled with the strings following his verbal commands his hands moved to my back. After a few minutes, his right hand slipped into my little girl ruffle underwear. I remember feeling a terrible emptiness in my stomach as I felt his hand move from my back into my underwear and sat directly on my bare skin. An intense almost electric feeling ran through my body. It was a feeling I didn't recognize or knew what to do with. I immediately jumped up and made up an excuse to go run home. The rest is a blur...I don't remember the excuse, what I did when I ran home however, that feeling is one of the most intense memories I carry in by soul. It would be the first of many encounters with men who would see me as prey and carry out full attacks on my body and soul like vultures. I was not prepared for what life had in store for me; this was just the beginning. I recall the tears that ran down my face during that session. Warm tears that carried a lifetime of heartache, shame, and guilt—the guilt a girl feels after a man violates her; the guilt society puts on women and girls with every occasion of being less than or being deserving of the violence imposed on our bodies. I remember how frightening it was to let that pain peek out for those few minutes. The fear was that once it came out, I might never have the strength to put it away again. But I was able to set it aside and go about my day as if nothing happened. The many years of compartmentalizing in order to survive paid off.

Sandi would often ask me if I would be okay to return to the office since my sessions were during lunch, and I always assured her that by the time I stepped out of the elevator, I'd be completely fine. I was usually fine by the time I got to the office across the street. It was my superpower and my biggest weakness; I could remove my mind and heart from any situation. My body could be in a room while any of my abusers declared full war on me, but my mind ran leaving my physical being to receive whatever wrath would be imposed upon it.

Therapy continued to be a safe place where I visited a painful past and attempted to understand an uncertain present. I would go on to explore the single most painful event of my lifetime. The one event that changed me forever, even more so than all the abuse of every man in my life. It created a scar that never healed. It filled me with pain that radiated through my mind with every heartbeat. It would be the focus of my therapy over the next twelve months. It would shake me to my core and challenge my entire existence. It would be the pinnacle moment that would change the course of not just my life but also the life of my five children, my abusive husband, my mother, sister, brother, and father. Being able to finally heal from this event would be just as impactful as the event was in ways I would never be prepared to understand.

The results from therapy were subtle; it was a long time before I realized I was changing. One of the most enlightening moments was when Sandi told me that I wasn't responsible for my husband's health or moods. It was the first step in the right direction since I still felt responsible for all of his feelings, both positive and negative. It would be years before I would allow myself to give up that responsibility.

Attempting to control the outcome of every event had been part of my life for many years. I can't pinpoint the moment it started, but I do know that the constant chaos in my life was likely the trigger. I can recall chaos going back to my parents' separation when my father left and my mother started to relive the youth she never had. The element of uncertainty and instability became part of my mind and body so early in life that I didn't know that it wasn't normal. In 1981, when I was eight and we moved to America, I experienced the loss of everything I knew for a new life where my feelings played an insignificant role. The changes were happening at such a fast pace that all I could do was cope. Trying to control the outcome of life would become my biggest challenge and most ambitious goal.

My need for control would affect all my relationships, particularly those with my children. I learned that my self-imposed judgment, self-hatred, and insecurities would morph into my children's personalities and cause their own attempts to control their surroundings. It is a vicious cycle that goes back generations. The sad part of being an individual with these struggles is that there are never enough successes or achievements to create self-love. It is only learning where these coping mechanisms come from and healing that helps achieve the elusive self-love so many boast about. My children became victims as I attempted to control them in an effort to give my husband that happiness I thought I owed him. In my damaged mind, his happiness would result in love for me.

In therapy, we explored my memories, feelings, and struggles. For some time, I became hyper-focused on the unfairness of the world and, particularly, my struggles in my career. I would spend hour upon hour until I reached exhaustion talking about my experiences with sexism, racism, and unfair treatment of others. Sandi commented one day that I was willing to advocate for others but not for myself. It was another moment of clarity. I went on to realize that advocating for myself, regardless of its merit, felt selfish and therefore shameful. It was another symptom of self-loathing: I wasn't deserving of being fought for, but others were. I'd be willing to fight for others to the point where I often feared for my job, but I would not put up that fight for myself. It took years before I would take steps to protect myself from sexist or racist comments from my colleagues or other business associates. It would take even longer for me to fight for fair pay. I remember the first moment I stood up for myself was when a business associate made an inappropriate comment about a female coworker and, instead of laughing with the group the way I'd been taught, I condemned the comment. I felt as though I'd taken back a speck of power.

My growth came in small increments. They were so subtle that I didn't even realize how I was changing. I remember once telling my husband that I felt empowered because I stood up to the family members who participated or knew about the life-changing event and didn't do anything. I recall feeling an internal strength that was foreign and new. His response was that he knew I'd leave him soon. I was puzzled by his response and went on to do what I did best, stroke his ego and reassure him until I felt he was satisfied. We had this same conversation several times over our last twelve months together. Now looking back, I realize that he saw I was changing before I did. He knew the abuse would have to come to an end soon.

Sandi challenged my thinking in the most-gentle ways. She would question my motives for decisions while reaffirming that I was free to make any decisions I felt good about. She would challenge my fears of my husband and my constant need to control my environment. She also prolonged moments when I felt pride and self-love, not allowing me to minimize my accomplishments and use self-deprecating language, as was my usual practice. My favorites criticisms were "I am not that smart" or "I am not special". It was extremely uncomfortable for me to sit in those moments of pride and self-love. I felt arrogant and egotistical, which was followed by shame and guilt. The shame came from my need for acknowledgment and the guilt for enjoying it. It is such a vicious cycle to work so hard for acceptance and love from others while simultaneously feeling shameful for those needs. I would go on to learn that these were patterns of unconscious behavior I'd learned in my childhood. I also later recognized that I was teaching my own children the same self-destructive patterns. These patterns were a foundational aspect of the abusive relationships I'd had throughout life.

Sandi also helped me to recognize that I was a survivor of so much and I'd been living in survival mode my entire life. It wasn't until I felt that I'd reached a place of financial stability that I became cognizant of my mental health needs. I'd started to become aware of the lack of wellness I was experiencing while not understanding what it was. At the time, I didn't know that I lived in a constant state of anxiety and acute stress. I didn't understand that while I hated chaos in my life, I unconsciously sought it out in my relationships because it felt familiar. It would be years before I'd learn that violence, substance abuse, lack of boundaries, and neglect were not a normal part of other people's life experiences. I genuinely thought it was normal to live under such circumstances. It would also take me years to understand that all these things had been normalized to the point where I didn't realize how bad they were. I couldn't comprehend the gravity of abuse and how it impacts its victims physically, emotionally, and mentally. Abuse had deteriorated my body so much that I was experiencing pain at all times. I had been close to my breaking point so many times but somehow I'd managed to continue to fight even when I had nothing left in me.

### REFLECTIONS FROM RECOVERY

» Everyone needs mental health support. Tending to our mental health is as important as tending to our physical health because they work together and affect one another. Checking in on our mental health is as critical as getting a physical exam.

» Everyone's healing journey is different. Our trauma shows up and manifests in different ways so we need a different mixture of tools to dissolve it. Also, our readiness is different regardless of age or life experiences. It is our responsibility and most beneficial to try different methods that include therapy (individual and group), meditation, journaling, and medication. I do believe medication can be useful to regulate the nervous system while you do the work. The best way to start is by reading about trauma and mental health using formats that resonate with us. I started with therapy while also following educational people and organizations on social media, I later moved on to podcasts and finally books. The order in which I read the books was also helpful because one book prepared me for the next.

» We all have a breaking point or limited capacity however, it is different for everyone. Society has created many stigmas around substance abuse, anxiety, panic attacks, other forms of addiction and suicide as if they are a sign of weakness. However, the reality is that these are all manifestations of our individual breaking points just like physical limits. While one person can be an olympic athlete another one can have a heart attack from running. The difference between those two individuals may be body composition, nutrition, preparation, or lifestyle. We don't necessarily assume that one individual is better, we typically see a heart attack as a sad occurrence not a sign of weakness.

» Trauma may be caused by big and small events. Trauma is an event that threatens our safety in any way. For example, a big event is physical violence in the home. Once we have been physically threatened in our home by a parent we will never feel safe while that parent is around. An example of a small event is being bullied in the playground during our early school years. Although a physical threat didn't exist the child felt unsafe to be themselves, felt a form of rejection and lack of emotional safety. Unless someone helped the child deal with the threat in either scenario a trauma may form. The majority of society has some form of unresolved trauma because many of our parents weren't equipped to help us navigate those experiences or regulate emotionally.

## RECOMMENDED RESOURCES AND INFORMATION

The books I read in the order I read them. I will say that Gabrielle Bernstein's books are absent of the experiences unique to minority groups. *What Happened to You* and *How to Do the Work* do acknowledge the additional traumas associated with being a POC.

» *What Happened to You* by Oprah Winfrey and Dr. Bruce D. Perry
» *The Universe Has Your Back* by Gabrielle Bernstein
» *Happy Days* by Gabrielle Bernstein
» *How to Do the Work* by Dr. NiDylan LePera

## Chapter 2 - The Final Push

The first hurdle to overcome in therapy was my husband at the time and everything we had gone through. When I met Kevin, I was thirty-five years old but felt like I was fifty from carrying so much emotional weight and a lifetime of survival. Being in a constant state of survival meant I wasn't living at all. I, of course, had no idea that was happening. All I knew was that I had surpassed my initial goal of getting off public assistance and was now moving into new territory of what seemed like more. I was determined to keep moving forward as far as I could go. After leaving my first husband, Johnny, I constantly reminded myself that I was given a second chance at life and had to make the best of it. I felt an immense sense of responsibility to give my kids more than I had. I never thought about wealth, I just wanted them to have a real childhood, a safe home, and their basic needs met—that was more than I had. Unfortunately, although I had gone through some therapy while I was with Johnny and immediately after I left him, I never really resolved any of my trauma.

Kevin was a master at studying people and finding their weaknesses. Also, I was an open book with a strong willingness to be vulnerable in an attempt to connect—so he really didn't have to try very hard. I had been single for over a year and was feeling really lonely. In retrospect, maybe he wasn't even that good at studying people. I gave him all he needed to know—and he knew just how to exploit it.

We met online. This was my first attempt at online dating, so I wasn't very good at it. He was only the fourth date I had gone on after weeks of browsing and chatting with men. I remember his profile said he was looking to meet people and make friends, which was odd for a dating site. Still, he was attractive, available, and local according to the app.

We met for lunch on a Friday for our first date at some fast food spot in Manhattan. He was extremely charming and made me laugh a lot. I didn't know how to differentiate between nerves, fear, and excitement back then—and I am still learning how to tell the difference now. I asked him to have dinner with me the same day, and we essentially stayed together from that day forward.

During the first few months, we were almost never apart. We commuted together, drank almost daily, and hung out all the time—partly because of the holidays, and partly because I was so glad to have an adult to talk to that seemed to understand my career struggles. I didn't really have anyone who could relate to my views about the system, being a disenfranchised person, and corporate America. We would spend hours talking about these things, which fulfilled a part of me that was just starting to awaken—my passion for social justice.

We decided to train together for a marathon, which gave us an excuse to move in together. He was living at a friend's house at the time, so it didn't take much effort. We ran our first joint marathon in April of 2009. It was a terrible experience for me; however, getting through it made me feel incredibly accomplished. Immediately afterward, the dynamics within the household quickly began to shift into a power struggle. Looking back, it is so clear that he was attacking every part of me he was jealous of. I can now see clearly how inadequate I made him feel, and how he needed to compensate for that by making me feel inferior. I already had unhealed childhood trauma that made me susceptible to abuse, so it was easy for him to exploit that and make me feel less than. I felt a constant unconscious need to prove I was good enough. The more he criticized me and told me I was a bad mother or bad partner, the harder I worked to be better. It was a perfect disaster.

We'd only been together a few months when I found out I was pregnant in May of 2009 while I was dealing with a huge project at work. I was trying extremely hard to continue to make my way at work while dealing with an increasingly abusive relationship at home. Still, my fear of abandonment outweighed my fear of abuse. I had lived with domestic violence all my life, so the emotional abuse I was experiencing felt like a very normal part of any romantic relationship. This prompted me to work harder to earn his love, fix him, and create the family I wish I had as a child. When I told him I was pregnant, I said I would have an abortion if he didn't want to have the baby, but then we had to break up. I am not sure if that was my way of keeping him, or if it was the guilt I felt over the abortions I had as a teenager.

When I was ten weeks along, I took my three kids to the grocery store while Kevin stayed home and painted. On the way, I realized I had forgotten something, and came back home to pick it up. I sent Kari in to get it; however, she returned a few minutes later saying Kevin wouldn't let her in the house. I barged upstairs to an overwhelming smell of weed. When I walked into the bedroom to question him about it, I realized he was watching porn on the computer. I was livid for many reasons, but mainly over the type of porn that he was watching—it featured girls rather than women. It triggered all of my childhood trauma associated with sexual abuse. That was the first night he physically hurt me.

After hours of arguing in our bedroom, the argument moved to the bathroom where he choked me. As we continued to argue because I didn't believe his explanation of how that type of porn popped up, I turned quickly to walk past him toward the bathroom door. He immediately wrapped his hand around my throat and pinned me against the wall, picking me up off the ground slightly. It lasted long enough to scare me in a whole new way. He choked me for enough time that I started to struggle and feel a lack of oxygen to my brain. It was like diving too far down into a pool, and the desperation you feel when you can see the light at the surface but it seems like you won't make it up in time to catch your breath before you pass out. I hadn't felt that type of fear in years—not since Johnny—and it sent me spinning.

He finally let me go when I looked into his eyes and repeatedly told him he was hurting me. The argument went on for over twelve hours until I conceded that I was wrong. Well into the morning, I noticed I didn't have any morning sickness and wondered why, but I was too tired to give it too much thought. Three days later, I went to the doctor and found out I had lost the baby. I was devastated in a way I'd never been before. Having babies was one thing I was really good at. I was abused during all of my previous pregnancies, so why did I lose this baby? I became obsessed with the miscarriage. I felt broken and even less worthy of love. I never blamed him out loud. Instead, I blamed myself and tried to find an explanation that didn't point back at my defective body.

I was in a deep depression over the next few months. On July 7, my thirty-sixth birthday, Kevin proposed in the car while driving home from work. I accepted;

although deep inside, I knew it was a mistake. I was in denial, but I knew the violence would continue as it had since that first day he choked me. He'd become increasingly jealous and insecure. I imagine the more abusive he became, the more insecure he was—and so the cycle was full on. He would become jealous, I would become defensive, he would abuse me, and then he would promise me the moon and the stars. My typical response to these interactions was to try to please him and avoid triggering him. I absorbed all the blame and put in even more effort to earn his love in hopes that he wouldn't hurt me anymore.

We were married by September of that same year, and by October, I was expecting Kyle. Kevin was extremely physically and emotionally abusive during the first eight years of the marriage; however, that pregnancy was especially difficult. The emotional abuse he unleashed on me during those nine months was far more damaging than the physical abuse. He cut off all physical affection and romantic interactions, leaving me completely emotionally stunted. I felt alone, unlovable, and completely abandoned. Sex had been the only way we connected since he was not emotionally available, so cutting off sex at that incredibly vulnerable time was devastating to me. I continued working throughout the pregnancy, commuting into the city and dealing with his extreme abuse while attempting to raise my other children. Looking back, I don't know how I survived through all that pain and pressure. It was incredibly difficult to be rejected by my partner while pregnant, particularly since I already had so many body image and self-worth issues.

The violence progressed along with the constant strain in the household. One night, while I was crying and complaining about his lack of affection or interest in me, he lost it. I was at least six months pregnant at the time. We were lying next to each other, and after several minutes of me crying and pressuring him for an answer as to why he wouldn't come near me, he went off. He started yelling until I brought up his porn addiction since that was an ongoing theme in our marriage, then he sprung up, sat on top of me, and choked me. It was incredibly scary lying there on the bed with his weight on me. I struggled while he pressed harder on my throat. Eventually, I was able to get out a few words to reason with him, and he let me go.

This same scenario happened once again after Kyle was born, except that time he choked me harder and I struggled for much longer. He had taken Sebastian to baseball practice, and I was on his computer. In the web history, I saw that he had been watching porn and looking through personal ads for sex on Craigslist. When he got home, I confronted him and we got into a huge fight. That fight was way more violent and he held me down for a really long time. These fights that led to me being held down and choked caused years of PTSD for me.

A partner with a porn addiction—or one on a constant search for other partners—has an enormous effect on a partner with sexual abuse trauma. When a woman grows up feeling as though her worth is associated with her sexuality and appearance, having a partner who seeks visual satisfaction through porn is devastating. It reinforces the idea that she isn't good enough to sexually satisfy her partner, leaving her with nothing. I felt completely worthless, and he knew it. I don't know if he ever actually cheated on me, but he didn't have to. The damage was deep and it cut through to my very core, reopening all my old wounds. It left me with a deep need to be chosen.

Kevin's violence continued throughout our relationship and spilled onto the kids. He was particularly violent with Sebastian but not exclusively; he had his moments with the girls as well. He had convinced me that what he was doing was right because boys needed a stronger hand. One of his many arguments when I became protective of the kids was that I didn't know what it was like to have a father. He argued that his father raised him and his sister with a strong hand and they turned out well. He repeatedly told me I was too soft on the kids—and I believed him.

I was so afraid of parenting like my mother and sister that I was determined to do whatever it took to provide a better home life for my family. I didn't understand that the lack of boundaries and the constant violence in my life were the real problems. It was hard to know what I needed to do differently when I didn't understand what was wrong to begin with. The violence continued for many years, although it became less frequent as time passed. I think the frequency changed because he had so many of us to abuse, he didn't need the violence to feel the adrenaline rush, and we offered fewer opportunities as we learned how to maneuver around him.

With Dylan, my pregnancy was much easier. I cared less, I was almost done with school, and my responsibilities at work had grown to a point where I had less room to entertain him. Having been through this before, I had prepared myself emotionally and was able to detach, especially with so many other things to focus on. Being financially independent became my number one goal. I needed to provide for my children financially since I couldn't give them the love they deserved and the safety they needed. I was struggling to try to finish my master's program. My physical health became compromised a number of times. I realize now that my body was sounding the alarm, but I didn't hear it. I was in a hypervigilant state all the time. I was under constant attack by my partner, I was raising kids that were the product of an unsafe environment, my family was a source of constant triggers and repressed trauma, and I was under a great deal of pressure at work. Life was really hard for a long time, and my body was taking the brunt of the attack.

I finished my master's program after Dylan was born, which I thought would get me to a place of feeling like I was finally worthy of love—but it didn't. I still felt like I wasn't good enough for anyone, especially for myself. Now, I understand that my wounds were so deep that the more hurt I experienced at home and work, the harder I worked to be accepted and loved by others; but, in reality, I needed to learn to love and accept myself. It was the deep-rooted shame and guilt I carried from all the sins that had been committed against me that didn't allow me to see my own worth. I couldn't see that I was good enough without the extra accomplishments, the right appearance, running marathons, raising five kids, or pleasing everyone. I couldn't see that just being a human was enough. I couldn't see that, just like my kids, I deserved my own love because, like them, I too was a blessing. I saw myself as a sin—dirty, needy, insignificant. "Too much" is how I often felt about myself. Like I was asking for far too much by asking for respect and love.

My home life continued unchanged. The more I accomplished, the more he grew to hate me. He lied and said he loved me, but if only I would do these few things so he wouldn't have to get angry.... It was palpable at times, and I even told him on occasion that it felt as though he hated me. That would trigger him to work harder to hide it. It was all very temporary, and it would usually push him to unleash on my kids instead.

In 2015, I went on a work trip with three colleagues who I considered close friends. We had a presentation to give at our parent company, and as per usual, we nailed it. On the two-hour train ride home, Kevin was harassing me about Sebastian and some insignificant thing he'd done. It was Kevin's way of getting attention because I was out accomplishing things on my own while he was sitting at home doing nothing. It was infuriating to have to deal with this level of harassment, and since I wouldn't agree with the severe punishment he wanted to administer, he wouldn't back down.

I was both embarrassed and exhausted, and for the first time in the seven years we'd been together, I said he was abusive out loud. I told my colleagues that he was abusive and that I was tired. They listened and empathized without judgment. Now that it was out in the universe, I could see it for what it was. I finally started bringing up therapy; however, he wasn't buying it.

What actually brought it all to a head was when I caught him once again engaging with strangers in inappropriate conversations. This time it was a young woman at Rutgers University who was almost the same age as my college-age daughter. It sent me into a rage, and if there was one thing I learned from my mother, it was that you don't leave a man for abuse, but you do leave him for cheating. I finally told him the only option was couples therapy, and he agreed as he knew he'd pushed me too far. The fights over the cheating had also escalated the violence as it triggered my abandonment wounds. It got to the point where the periods of calm in between the storms were almost nonexistent. There was always something happening at home. I felt as though I was drowning all the time. I felt his hands around my throat choking me just enough to keep me in a constant state of fear.

This all happened in December of 2015, which was the busiest time of year at work. I was overseeing huge projects that challenged me every day. My body reacted to what was happening in a way that I hadn't experienced in many years. I stopped eating and sleeping but continued to exercise and work without interruption. I lost a ton of weight and felt desperate. It was a scary time.

The more we went to therapy, the more Kevin focused his anger on Sebastian since he was afraid to turn on me. We didn't talk about the physical abuse in therapy for a long time. We talked about verbal abuse and emotional abuse, but we skirted around the physical violence. Despite everything he'd done to me and my kids, I was still protecting him—a dynamic I learned in my childhood home. We never called the cops, we never reported it or even talked about it. This lesson was so deeply rooted inside me that here I was protecting my abuser, much like my family had protected my brother.

Eventually, I started mentioning the escalating "discipline" over the kids, particularly Sebastian, until one day the therapist said: "No more violence." It was such a relief to have someone validate my aversion to his version of "discipline". That was the most powerful accomplishment with this therapist. She gave me permission to stand my ground and not allow any more violence toward my kids or myself.

There were a few incidents during this time between Kevin and Bee. Bee was going through a rebellious period, partying and drinking quite a bit. One night she came home with a black eye, but wouldn't say what happened. Kevin became obsessed with trying to find out the story behind it. He learned that she had been at the a local bar, and called me at work to tell me. I told him not to confront her until I got home because I knew it wouldn't go well. But by the time I came home, Bee had a mark on her face. Kevin said he hadn't done anything, but my mom was there at the time and said he had grabbed Bee, though she didn't see the whole argument. Doing what I'd been taught, I didn't even ask Bee for her side of what happened. I just let it go.

Just weeks later, there was a second incident. He didn't like her tone of voice, and it escalated. During this incident, he went after her. When I walked into the room, he was grabbing her by the hair. I intervened and grabbed his forearm, my nails digging into his skin. He let go of her but grabbed me by the throat instead. He choked me for a minute or so while I struggled against him. The girls, Dylan, and Kyle all hid behind me screaming when Sebastian suddenly ran into the room. He started telling everyone to calm down and talk it out. Eventually, we negotiated that we would let go of each other simultaneously. I threatened to call the cops, but he responded that the evidence showed that I attacked him since my nails had pierced his skin and I didn't have any cuts. I believed him. He was an attorney and could probably manipulate the situation to tell whatever story he wanted. After this incident, I warned him to never touch any of my children again. He never did—although he tried extremely hard to trigger them at every opportunity.

A few months later, Bee ran away. I was devastated and overcome with fear for her wellbeing, not to mention riddled with guilt and shame. It was my fault she ran away, and honestly, I didn't blame her. I wanted to run away too. Kevin did everything in his power to isolate her and turn the kids and me against her. He treated her as though she'd personally betrayed him, as though she was his ally and had abandoned him during battle. I remember arguing with him and telling him that he acted like she'd committed a terrible crime. She was just a kid running from a terrible home. Secretly, I rooted for her and hoped she'd find peace. Unfortunately, she was really struggling, and I had no capacity to help her. This was the moment when Karinna suggested I find someone of my own to work with. I found Sandi that week.

It was in 2016 when Kevin finally pushed me too far—when he challenged Sebastian to a fight. He confronted Sebastian because he forgot to take out the garbage. It was in September, shortly after Sebastian turned eighteen and started his senior year of high school. I'd just walked in from work when Kevin noticed the garbage was full and called me and Sebastian into the kitchen. He yelled at Sebastian for a long time about laziness, disrespect, and a number of other inappropriate accusations. He got in Sebastian's face and told him to go outside and fight him like a man since Sebastian thought he didn't have to follow the rules. Sebastian had first apologized and said he forgot, but then kept quiet as his stepfather continued to berate and hurl accusations at him. I got in between them, and Kevin proceeded to call Sebastian a "pussy" and "mama's boy". The name-calling went on until I lost my temper and sent Sebastian to his room and argued with Kevin. I went to see a divorce attorney within a week.

I also spoke to a friend at work who'd experienced similar dynamics with his father. He helped me so much because I was in a complete state of panic. I was convinced Kevin wanted to hurt Sebastian, and I was afraid to go to work every day and leave him vulnerable. This friend helped me off the ledge and allowed me to see that getting out was possible.

Kevin realized he had gone too far when I told him I was filing for divorce. He enrolled in a six-month batterer's program and started going to therapy on his own. We were still seeing the couples therapist, but I realized she wasn't helping. In part, I felt constantly judged by her as we are minorities and she wasn't, and secondly, I wasn't seeing an improvement in our dynamic.

The attorney I hired in October filed for divorce in January of 2017. Unfortunately, by that point, I had noticed a significant difference in Kevin's behavior and decided to give him a second chance. I found a different therapist, a Black woman, who seemed to have a deeper understanding of our struggles. Suddenly, Kevin was a completely different person. He was calm, kind, and thoughtful. Suddenly he cared about the kids and made kind gestures toward them, which warmed my heart. He had also become kind and patient with me, stopped raising his voice, was supportive, and really listened to me. It was as though I existed as a person again. It felt so good to be seen and heard after such a long time of being made to feel as if I didn't matter. I could not believe that the program had actually worked. We talked about the program and the lessons he'd learned. How he could see the wrong in his behavior and how he wanted to be this new person he was becoming. I felt so much hope. I wholeheartedly believed in his new commitment to our family and relationship. I was all in again.

I returned to school for my doctorate after many couples therapy sessions where we discussed how he would support me. He promised to help more around the house and with the kids. He assured me that the violence was behind us. He agreed to put in more effort so I wouldn't feel so alone and overburdened all the time. Initially, he helped by preparing dinners since he got home about two hours before I did. He cleaned up toys and helped with the laundry. He shopped for groceries and interacted with the older kids without being mean or attacking them. He helped me do our Christmas shopping and was more patient during our family vacation. He sent me sweet texts and worried about my wellbeing. His commitment lasted for some time, about six months of full effort before I started noticing the subtle changes.

At some point, couples therapy had become obsolete. We were thriving as a family. Bee became pregnant, and although she and her high school boyfriend, Alex, were only twenty-one, Kevin was supportive of my decision to help them. He showed kindness toward Kari and treated her well. Even Sebastian was met with a more receptive version of a man who once showed hatred toward him. It seemed as though we had nothing left to talk about in therapy because Kevin reported complete satisfaction and I was happy with his changes. He had become the man he once promised he would be, and I finally felt safe. All my sacrifices and dedication were paying off, and he was able to see my worth and love me. A man loved me unconditionally even though he knew I wasn't perfect. I was worthy of love and kindness. This newly found peace allowed me to focus on my own recovery. I was finally able to spend more time working through my childhood trauma during individual therapy now that my family life seemed settled.

Eventually, home life started to slip. Kevin's involvement with the boys became less and less. The unpredictable irritability showed up unexpectedly, and he became less present with each day. Pretty soon we were back to tiptoeing around him. Still, I was so consumed by motherhood, my career, school, and my desperate need to have a stable family that I explained everything away. So much of our abusive relationship was familiar that I didn't know how to gauge the success of this "healthy" version of us.

I remember once telling Sandi that I wanted to allow Sebastian to move back in when the girls moved out. She asked me why I didn't do it, and I explained that it would make Kevin angry. She asked if Kevin and I had discussed it, and I said no. When she asked why not, I said that I was worried about how he would react. She told me that being fearful of a conversation was not a sign of a healthy relationship. She explained that we should be able to talk about anything even if it made one of us upset. It was a moment of awakening for me. I had no idea that was how relationships worked. I genuinely believed that avoiding difficult situations and feeling hurt about it was normal.

Sandi and I continued to have those moments where I learned what seemed like small obvious truths about myself, relationships, and healthy patterns I knew nothing about. By 2019, Kevin was practically back to himself. He was completely emotionally unavailable while becoming more aggressive. He was yelling and cursing at me over everything and anything. Our fights would end with him physically intimidating me, although he didn't choke me. He didn't actually have to touch me; I was so afraid of violence that I typically shut down once I felt threatened. I tried really hard to hold on to hope by giving him more and more with the goal of making him happy so he could be the man I loved. I gave him more freedom, more money, more space, but nothing worked. He was just returning to the incredibly unhappy man who hurt me in a million ways.

In September, he became irate because Kari ate a bag of potato chips that he liked. When he brought up the issue with me, I responded that we will just buy more. He went off about her lack of consideration for others and how rude she was. I wouldn't back down as I could see through his bullshit. He just wanted an excuse to fight, but I refused to give in. He then changed his tactic and challenged my concern about her eating disorder. That was his way of making me feel like a bad parent and setting himself up as the thoughtful, caring stepfather. I replied no, that it was her birthday, and she ate a bag of chips, so who cares. I went on to point out that he was being manipulative and questioned why he was trying so hard to start a fight. Was it about Kari, me, or himself? He eventually stormed off, and I made a mental note of it.

These types of interactions continued with some frequency. We argued because he couldn't find his socks. We argued because he canceled our family vacation as we were getting ready to leave. We argued because I was texting too much with my coworkers and he was jealous, although it was nothing new. It quickly became clear that he wanted to find any possible excuse to argue. I worked harder and harder to ignore it while making mental notes of the changes. We were now back to our old dynamic where I was getting minimal help with the family. He was laser-focused on his own goals and clearly not interested in a relationship that required mutual effort and, most of all, respect.

My schooling was mostly online; however, I had a residency per year to attend. In early October, I had an eleven-day residency in Arizona, which meant two additional days of travel. I would be gone for almost two weeks, the longest I'd ever been away from Kevin or any of my kids. I was super excited as this residency marked the beginning of the last year of my program. I loved what I was learning and I felt as though I was finally figuring out my direction. For the first time, I was doing something because I wanted to not because I had to. I planned every aspect of my absence with my daughters who would fill in for me. They planned the boys' weekend meals, transportation to and from school, and childcare. Kevin's only responsibility in my absence was to be home at night while the boys slept.

While I was nervous, I was mostly excited to embark on this new adventure as a college student without kids, a demanding husband, or work. I would fully immerse in the college experience for an entire thirteen days. I still dealt with a little bit of work and some minor kids stuff, but I mostly just did schoolwork and spent time with my classmates. It felt glorious.

Then one night, my classmates and I decided to go out to eat instead of eating at the hotel. We went to a nearby restaurant where we had a few drinks and tons of laughs. As it got later, Kevin kept texting me because he knew I was out. He became more and more irate with each text and finally FaceTimed me. I answered the phone while in the car with my classmates. It didn't go well, and it was obvious to everyone in the car. I felt like the high school girl who dates insecure men who always go after younger girls because they can't handle adult women. He scolded me, then hung up on me in a temper tantrum.

I had two more days of classes before I would fly back home on a red-eye. While sitting in the classroom during a lecture, Bee called me repeatedly. My granddaughter, Kalani, who was only one year old had fallen at the park and was in the emergency room. I reached out to Kevin, Kari, and Sebastian to go find out what was happening and asked them to keep me informed. At some point, while the baby was being checked and some people were in the waiting room, Kevin felt he'd been slighted because no one was paying attention to him. He sent a text to the family chat chastising the kids, saying that if I were there they would prioritize me and keep me informed, and accusing them of being rude. He did this while the baby was still in the ER. That text triggered me in a way I'd never recognized before. It was a new sense of self-awareness like nothing I'd ever experienced.

I asked Sandi for a phone session because I was experiencing an immense emotional charge. I was outraged by his audacity to attempt to make that moment about him while my granddaughter was hurt. He created hostility at a moment when the entire family was having an emotional crisis. He wanted to pay me back for my outing by abusing the kids when they were vulnerable. I didn't understand his intentions at the time, but my body was reacting and I felt it. What became clear to me was that I felt calm while at school and his threat toward my kids sent me into a whirlwind of distress. I realized for the first time that I lived in a constant state of fear and it wasn't normal.

When I returned, we argued about the incident for a while but didn't get anywhere and left it for a few days. I needed to focus on my work and the kids. I recall one evening when he asked me in detail about my trip and I told him how amazing the experience was. I expressed clarity and feeling empowered. I also explained that cutting my family off helped me find my way and see my vision. He responded by saying he would be cut off next. I, of course, responded, "not unless you hurt me again." He obviously saw the writing on the wall before I did. He knew I'd changed over the past few years and was finally reclaiming my power.

I told him that we had to go back to therapy immediately because I was at the end of my rope. We were back in therapy within days. At our first session back, he lied regarding an episode of violence against Sebastian, and that was it for me. I'd had enough; I declared right there that it was over. We sat in the car arguing for hours after the session. He insisted that it wasn't his fault, he didn't lie, he didn't start with the kids, he didn't abuse me—but eventually said he was sorry and would do anything to fix it. I already knew it was over and I would do anything to get myself and my kids away from this hellhole of a man. The divorce conversation began again, and so did his constant vacillation between kindness and extreme abuse. He waged a full war on my mind and body, but it would manifest in small constant battles driving me to my breaking point.

November was particularly strenuous in the house. The holidays were around the corner and we were at full-on war. Kevin would not let up, and I could feel my body prepare as I got closer to home each day after work. Sometimes, he would call me during the ride leaving me zero space to feel safe. I had only told Kari at this point. She was the oldest, most emotionally mature, and seemed to understand the most about the dysfunction. I later found out she called out sick from work the day I told her about the divorce because she was so overcome by anxiety. At this point, he was attempting to convince me to let him handle the divorce instead of hiring attorneys. I was actually considering it—until after I agreed to split all the assets, he asked me about alimony. I could not believe the nerve of this man who I'd financially supported for years. He couldn't keep a job, get any of the businesses he attempted off the ground, or help me run the household, and now he had the nerve to ask for money. I decided to use the attorney who represented me against Johnny when he attempted to get custody of the kids. She had changed my life once, and I was sure she would do it again—and this time, I could actually pay her.

I decided it was time to start gathering information, so I decided to look through his phone, which I hadn't done in years. I found evidence of several ongoing inappropriate interactions and relationships at work and on social media. This wasn't surprising, but it was triggering. We got into a big fight, and it led to him looking through my phone. I knew he often went through my stuff; however, I never said anything. This time, I didn't need to guess. It was as though a full-on tornado had been unleashed on me. He found a group chat between my classmates and me and a text chain with one male classmate, Greg. This classmate was also part of the group chat in which I'd told the group that although I just got As in both of the classes we just took, I was taking a leave of absense. I explained that I was having marital issues and needed time off to sort things out. Greg reached out directly to ask if I was okay and called me. We talked, and I told him just a little bit about what going on, and he gave me some moral support. That was enough to set Kevin off.

As I was getting the boys ready for bed, he started his verbal attack. He made assertions about an affair or inappropriate behavior while also calling me names. I attempted to defend myself but quickly stopped engaging as the boys were listening. I finished putting them to bed and went up to my room. Suddenly from upstairs, I could hear him on the phone. He was interrogating Greg and asking things like "why are you checking up on my wife?" and "does your wife have male friends?" It was embarrassing but also scary since I knew Kevin was very reactive. I could tell he'd lost control and would come after me now. He had not physically assaulted me in several years, although he'd become more physically intimidating recently. I felt that this was a pivotal moment that might end with my death, so I decided to record the confrontation. Four hours of name-calling, threats, and demeaning comments about all my insecurities; of him vacillating between crying, screaming, and breaking my property ensued.

It felt as though it would never end, but it did, as all things do. I remember telling myself that it would pass and end one way or another. I kept reminding myself that I've been through worse and nothing lasts forever. He left me alone and came back several times as I moved to different locations of the house to motivate an end and avoid the boys witnessing anything. The next day was Thanksgiving, so even with no sleep, I cooked and pretended everything was fine during the family dinner with all five kids and their respective partners. The weekend continued in the same vein as I felt unsafe and knew Kevin was unpredictable. He spent the weekend apologizing and trying to get my laptop fixed since he'd broken it during his temper tantrum.

That recording served me well. Listening to it after the fact helped me relive the event. I'd been disassociated most of the time and didn't understand the full magnitude of what happened. It also helped my therapist understand who I was dealing with, and it is now part of the divorce discovery.

Once I realized divorce was the only option, it took all of my courage to file. I knew it would be a long, traumatic, and risky process. His wrath was like nothing I could ever muster in terms of anger or revenge. His ability to be hurtful, spiteful, and ruthless outdid me every day. Also, that is just not the person I was or wanted to be. I would be putting myself and my children at risk for more pain and trauma, but I knew it was the best long-term plan. They would endure much more pain and trauma if I stayed with him. Creating a safe space for them to heal would be more beneficial than avoiding the hardship of the divorce. I was playing the long game. Of course, I didn't anticipate it would take quite so long.

It took about two and a half years to finalize the divorce. We had at least five court appearances, five mediation sessions, and many other dealings through the attorneys. He manipulated the system, lied in every setting, and attacked me at every opportunity. In the beginning, any communication from him was extremely triggering. His texts, emails, face, and anything about him sent me spinning and deregulated my nervous system. Granted, my nervous system was completely damaged and I had PTSD making me very vulnerable to triggers even if we didn't interact in person. It took a long time before I would feel safe in my body or home.

I learned about self care and began another part of my healing journey. Healing from childhood trauma, generational trauma, domestic abuse and survival mode are all different healing journeys that can happen simultaneously or separately. As Sandi and I have continued to work on all of these, I have learned that they often intersect but show up differently. There is no formula or easy fix, the work can be overwhelming and growling at times, however giving up all the heavy loads is incredibly freeing. I continue to work towards understanding who I was before all the trauma forced me to create coping mechanisms that became part of me. I am constantly shedding the parts of me that no longer serve me while choosing the parts that I love.

Aside from all the healing and trauma-related lessons I learned during this process, I was also reminded of how poorly the judicial system is set up to help victims. I always imagined that the reason I had such poor experiences in the past was because of my financial situation or my zip code. Essentially, I associated my poor experiences with living in an urban community, being a minority woman, and being in poverty. However, today, I am still a minority woman, and I now have the financial means and live in the suburbs, yet my abuser still has the access and opportunity to be abusive. I have had to file several motions regarding his constant violations of our civil restraint agreement. We had a parent coordinator, who was paid a lot of money, who was also overwhelmed by his abusive behavior. It seemed as though even the attorneys and the judge were somehow affected by his behavior. The disappointing part is that these individuals should be trained to understand domestic violence but rarely are. They can't seem to see the cycles of abuse, symptoms of abuse, or coping mechanisms victims rely on to survive. They don't understand that once the power dynamic has been established, victims don't see an out; that abusers know what triggers their victims' nervous systems; and that they will use physical and verbal intimidation at every opportunity.

A divorce is a major life event—much like a death. We have to grieve our dreams, hopes, and unkept promises. We have to feel the loss and the birth of a new life. We have to allow ourselves to find happiness within ourselves and learn to love ourselves unconditionally. The blame and disappointment naturally turn inward along with the guilt. I felt terrible guilt for over a year every time I saw the pain that was inflicted on my kids either by him or by the circumstances. It took me a long time to learn that giving them a safe space to be themselves and feel loved all the time was the best gift I could give them. It was the life they should have had, and they would have to learn to cope with a toxic father.

At the end of it all, after hours of therapy, journaling, mediation, and exercise pondering on the event, I came out a survivor. I do think that the extended time helped me more than it hurt me. It bought me the time to heal, process, grieve, and recover. I learned so much about my trauma, coping mechanisms, and who I really am. It took so much work to find myself again and to remember who I was…a little girl who was full of life, confidence, and deeply believed in love. In divorcing him, I chose to love me. I will give myself what I have been desperately looking for my entire life—not money, not protection, just love and acceptance. I am grateful for who I am and who I've always been.

### REFLECTIONS FROM RECOVERY

» Therapy validates the experiences of abuse victims, which is critical since most abusers minimize their victims' experiences. When the abuser or family members constantly tell the victim they are overreacting, the victim stops trusting their own judgment. Lack of self trust is a difficult concept to recognize. It can start in childhood when our parents minimize our experiences and we carry that into our romantic relationships. This works in the favor of the abuser who will reinforce that you're overreacting and that what they did wasn't that bad. The first thing therapy does is validate the pain, frustration, anger or sadness you feel is normal and expected. The goal is to eventually trust your own judgment again however, that takes time.

» Narcissism is a personality disorder (NPD) in which a person has an inflated sense of self-importance. Symptoms include an excessive need for admiration, disregard for others' feelings, an inability to handle criticism, and a sense of entitlement. (mayoclinic.com) NPD is rarely diagnosed because narcissists are often charming liars that do not recognize they need help.

» Admitting out loud that you are experiencing abuse is the first step. Each time I was in an abusive relationship, I felt great shame and guilt, which made it

harder to say it out loud. Yet, when I finally admitted it, I felt a weight lifted off of me, and it helped me start down the path to finding a way out.
- Staying in an abusive relationship doesn't make you weak, it just means you may have unresolved trauma. The abuse of the relationship typically feels familiar because it has similarities to a relationship from our childhood. Oftentimes, the relationship mimics the one between our parents or between one of our parents and ourselves. It feels like home, even though it is painful and scary, making it much harder for us to leave. The relationships we unconsciously seek are not always physically abusive but lead us to self-betrayal until we identify and resolve the trauma.
- Cascading trauma is when a person experiences new trauma on top of unresolved trauma. For example, dealing with domestic violence, food insecurity, and racism are a form of cascading trauma. Cascading trauma is overwhelming and requires slow, deliberate, and focused work. It requires identifying and working through each trauma using the tools available.
- PTSD is real and can affect domestic violence, sexual assault, and childhood trauma victims. We often associate it with soldiers; however, it is much more common than we think. Therapists have different tools available to treat PTSD.

## RECOMMENDED RESOURCES AND INFORMATION
**Domestic Violence:**
- Love Life Now Foundation, Inc. – Year-round Domestic Violence Awareness
- Domestic Violence Support | The National Domestic Violence Hotline (thehotline.org)
- Resources (ncadv.org)
- Resource Centers | The Administration for Children and Families (hhs.gov)

**PTSD:**
- Post-traumatic stress disorder (PTSD) - Symptoms and causes - Mayo Clinic
- A Guide to Post-Traumatic Stress Disorder (domesticshelters.org)

## Chapter 3 - Death Seemed Imminent

After months of therapy sessions working through Kevin and the dysfunctional relationship I tried so hard to normalize, we got to my first husband. Johnny is the biological father of my oldest three children, and he's by far the most sadistic person I'd ever met. I was only nineteen when I met him. He was twenty-six with a million more years of life experience than I had. Johnny was very handsome and extremely charming. He was by far the smoothest, most unassuming man I had met up to that point in my life.

At that time, I was so incredibly lost. My sister and I were running an illegal gambling club out of a coffee shop in downtown Paterson. We worked for the local mafia, who were a bunch of small-time wannabes. I'd barely graduated high school—a feat I was proud of as I was the first and only one of my siblings to receive a high school diploma. I was dabbling with drugs and abusing alcohol in an attempt to numb the pain I had deep in my heart. I was desperately looking for the unconditional love I'd never known. I was reckless and irresponsible. I had no direction, no positive role models, and no vision of what a healthy life could possibly look like.

Johnny was well known by the Italians we worked for as he had a dark past, which I wouldn't learn about until much later. However, he didn't present himself as a mobster but instead as a jewelry salesman. We met when he came into our coffee shop to collect money from one of the guys we worked for. He would come by weekly and show me jewelry and chit-chat. He was quiet, a good listener, and a gentleman. He seemed mature and responsible as he was always focused on work in our early interactions. Eventually, our conversations became more flirtatious, and I became very interested in him—and he knew it. I bought a piece of jewelry from him, which guaranteed his weekly visit to collect money from me. I, in my own messy and lonely life, started to fall hard, even though I knew nothing about him—and he knew everything about me. Finally, after weeks of visits that had become daily, we agreed to go out on a date. I remember thinking that he was so different from all the loser hoodlums I knew. The guys I'd grown up with, particularly my last few years of high school, were mostly drug dealers in some capacity. Some sold in large quantities while others were street runners. But Johnny had what seemed like a real job. The world I was in at the time was full of much older men who attempted to prey on me constantly in addition to young street guys and a lifetime of abuse. I was extremely vulnerable, and I don't think that falling into Johnny's trap was avoidable at that point in my life.

By the time we had our first date, I was already full of hope for a new beginning with a man who would love me like no other—and a chance to get out of my house. I had recently turned twenty when we finally went out. He'd ask me to go to the movies, and we'd agreed that he would pick me up at my house. We drove around a little, and then he said it was too late for the movie, but he wanted a place to just talk. We ended up at a Marriott where he got us a room but repeatedly said that it wasn't to hook up. My expectations of men were so low and my experience so poor that I was scared but also flattered that he wanted to hang out with me that bad. Naïve didn't begin to describe my mindset. I remember how confusing the feelings of fear and excitement were, so I did what I knew best. After a few hours of talking, mostly me talking about my life, my feelings, and and my pain, and thinking he was an excellent listener and caring person, we had sex. In just one night, we built the foundation for our entire relationship.

We quickly became exclusive—or so I thought. Within weeks, we were spending all our free time together, and he was becoming more and more involved in my life. He was very elusive about his life, but I didn't see that as a red flag. I chalked it up to men just not being vocal or expressive. Truthfully, I was so desperate for love and an escape from my home life, I ignored a number of red flags.

Most of our "dates" were in hotel rooms, which I welcomed since it got me out of my house. Then it happened…he called me on my house phone in an irate state. He was screaming like a psychopath about some guy that I previously dated who he knew, and how dare I keep that from him. My response was that it was none of his business because I didn't know him when I dated the guy. He went on to call me names and hurled all kinds of insults at me. Eventually, he threatened to "fuck me up", so I hung up on him. He called back over and over. I picked up the first few times but then refused to pick up again. I was in a full panic because he sounded scary. I told my sister and mother what happened, but their responses were non-existent. He eventually showed up at my house with a long apology and assured me that I was right and it was none of his business. We watched a movie we'd rented on my mom's couch. Once the movie was over and he'd reassured me repeatedly that I had nothing to worry about, I agreed to go with him to return the movie. He drove to Blockbuster and had me get out and drop it off, which I did.

Once I got back into the car, he drove onto the highway. I recall looking out the passenger window wondering why he was headed in that direction when out of nowhere I felt his fist slam against my face. I recall my blood splattered on the glass and how much my head ached from hitting the window. It was the hardest I'd ever been hit by anyone and the most frightened I'd ever felt. I started to open my door—I guess I was going to jump out—but he sped up and leaned over to close the door. He explained in an eerily calm voice that I was stupid to think I would get away with what I did. He said that I needed to learn my lesson, called me a whore, spit on my face, and said other horrible things while he drove to a town I wasn't familiar with.

During that twenty-minute ride, he was mostly silent. He hit me a few more times but not as hard as the first time—or maybe I was more prepared for them. After each hit, he'd calm down for a while. The car would become silent with only music playing in the background, then he'd start talking again. He would start off slow, explaining how much he loved and cared for me and how much it hurt to hear some guy tell him we'd dated. As he spoke, I could hear the tempo in his voice go up. He would work his way up to a frantic state, calling me names and hurling other insults at me. Once he was in this state, the next hit would come shortly after. Eventually, he pulled into a ShopRite parking lot full of tractor trailers right off the highway in a secluded area. He pulled into a very dark space in between two trucks.

He spent the next few hours torturing me, working to intimidate me and teach me that he would show me no mercy. He wanted me to know that I could either work hard to earn his love or I would have to deal with his wrath. I truly didn't know what his limits were, if there were any at all. The mental agony was by far worse than the physical pain I would endure. He proceeded to beat me for at least an hour. He hit me so many times that I was sure he would kill me. It was the most violence I'd experienced firsthand, and it established his full dominance over me. I responded with complete and total submission.

During the beating, he called me names and said incredibly hurtful things. He recounted every shameful, intimate, and hurtful secret I'd ever told him. He reminded me of all my insecurities and the family dysfunction I'd entrusted him with. He made me feel like the least loveable or worthy person on this earth. He made me loathe myself. The physical torture he inflicted caused pain, scars, and fear while the emotional pain would devastate me for years to come.

The beating followed the same pattern as the car ride. He'd exhaust himself from hitting me, then he'd take time to recharge. He would stop at times and cry while listing all the reasons why he had to do this. He'd explain that it was my fault and how I'd left him no choice. Girls like me, he'd say, are the worst because we think that our looks and fake innocence make us special, but we aren't. We're actually the worst kind of people because we use our appearance to control and manipulate men. His arsenal of weapons was endless. His cruelty was his strength and brought him joy.

The moments of calm gave me hope that it would come to an end, but he was so unpredictable. I prayed so hard for a miracle. I was afraid to say anything because everything I said seemed to upset him even more. I would have said or done anything to earn his love and mercy. I just wanted to prove that he was wrong and that he could love and trust me because then it would end. He occasionally took me out and beat me against the car; it was easier to hit my body and choke me that way. I repeatedly thought about running, but the fear of his reaction if he caught me caused me to freeze. Finally, it ended abruptly. He just drove back and dropped me off at my mother's house, but not before threatening to hurt my family if I called the cops—but he knew no one would. He knew my family had a long history of domestic violence that never resulted in accountability by the abuser.

I walked into my mother's house exhausted and confused. My face was destroyed. I had two black eyes, my lips were cut and swollen, and my nose was swollen and bloody. My bloodshot eyes were practically closed, and every inch of my face was discolored. There were other parts of my body with similar damage, but nothing looked worse than my face. I recall my mother was pretty upset and my sister asked me if I wanted to call the cops. Of course, I said no and just sat in the shame and pain I felt in my soul. His cruel words rang in my ears, and my fear became paralyzing. His complete control over my mind and body was established that night.

The next twelve months were the most violent and brutal of the five years we were together. He would oscillate between prince charming and complete psychopath regularly.

Shortly after that first beating, a doctor had prescribed me pain medicine with codeine for a sinus infection. I decided I'd had enough and took a few at once in an attempt to overdose. Johnny found me unresponsive at my mother's house and took me to the emergency room. I spent about twenty-four hours in the hospital, and my family didn't even know what happened. I think my mother had completely given up on me by this point, and I had so much resentment and ill will towards her that I didn't care. Johnny took care of me for a few days while I recovered, making me even more emotionally dependent. He had saved my life—which he threw in my face any chance he got. I felt as though he was the only person who saw me, good or bad. I'd never witnessed a healthy adult relationship in my life, which left me with no map or guide. All I knew was abuse and violence, so this relationship felt pretty familiar; although, it was much worse than anything I'd seen before.

Within just a few months of dating, and of the first beating and my attempted suicide, I became pregnant. This new baby brought me so much hope. I believed that if I gave him a healthy, perfect baby, he would really love me and not want to hurt me again. Boy was I wrong. The pregnancy was horrific.

Johnny got us an apartment, and I landed a job as a teller at a nearby bank. I'd worked as a teller before the gambling club fiasco. I'd left the club months prior in order to satisfy his demands. His jealousy was out of control and it became all-consuming. He threw out all my clothes and bought me new ones that were much more conservative than anything I'd normally wear. I became completely isolated from all of my friends and family. He instigated fights between my sister and me to ensure I'd have no one to turn to. The more I was on my own, the more I became emotionally dependent on him. He'd go to extremes to keep ahold of me.

A few weeks into the new apartment, I found out he still had a relationship with the woman he'd fathered his first child with. I tried to leave him for the first time—without considering the consequences. I packed my stuff and left for my mother's house while he was out one night. He went ballistic; the usual nonstop calls fluctuated between pleas for our grand love and detailed threats of bodily harm. After a few days, when I was walking out of work and toward the bus stop, he pushed me into a car I'd never seen before. As he knew I would, I froze in fear. We spent hours in the car. Even though I was pregnant, he wouldn't let me leave to eat or even go to the bathroom. He just kept insisting that he loved me and I needed to come back to the apartment with him so we could be together.

It was about midnight by the time he drove back to the apartment. I'd been sitting in the car arguing and pleading with him to let me leave for about seven hours. Completely exhausted, hungry, and dying to use the bathroom, I just gave in and did what he told me. I walked into the apartment without making a scene and laid down to sleep. When I woke up the next morning, the bedroom door was locked from the outside.

He kept me locked in the room for three days, only letting me out to use the bathroom, at which point he stood in front of the open door. He finally agreed to let me go to work once I promised to get back together with him. Needless to say, I was fired when I returned to work. My employer was also tired of the drama. Johnny would sometimes appear in the walk-up lobby of the bank where I was a teller and watch me for hours. He'd take mental notes of what he considered overly friendly interactions: when I smiled for too long or seemed too pleased to see customers. I eventually stopped making eye contact with people and became very deliberate with my interactions with others. I was afraid all the time, even when he wasn't there. The rage he unleashed on me when he became jealous was like no other—it didn't matter that I was pregnant. I stopped fighting altogether during the beatings, focusing strictly on protecting my belly and repeatedly promising to do better.

My paranoia became affixed to my brain by an incident that happened later in the pregnancy. As I sat in his car waiting for him, I kicked a bag on the floor full of cassette tapes. Naturally, I thought they were mixed tapes as he was a big music fan and often had new random music to share. I pushed the first cassette into the car stereo, but there was no music. After a few seconds of silence, I heard my voice. I fast-forwarded the cassette in full panic as my heart raced at a million miles. How can he have a cassette of my phone conversation, I frantically wondered. I continued to listen to random sections. It was more telephone recordings of my sister, my mother, and myself. I played several cassettes from the bag, and they were all days and days of recordings. He'd been recording my mother's house phone activity for months. Instead of being outraged and confronting him for spying on me and my family, I was deathly afraid that he would find out that I was looking through things in his car.

Not long after, I ran off to Costa Rica to my father's house in an attempt to get away from Johnny. I had been there for a few weeks when one day as my stepsister and I returned from an errand, we saw a rental car parked in front of my father's house. I said jokingly, "Imagine if that was Johnny," and we both laughed. We did think it was strange that this car was sitting there, but we continued into the house. When I walked in, I almost threw up. Johnny was sitting on the couch talking to my dad in broken Spanish. My dad immediately jumped up and raved about how much Johnny loved me to travel so far to propose. He'd asked my father for my hand in marriage, and my dad had agreed—even though he knew Johnny was abusive. My dad told me that my choices were limited since I was pregnant. Not surprising coming from the first man I'd experienced domestic violence from. I was told to just get back together with him and make it work. I had received similar advice from my mother, who once told me that Johnny beat me because I curse and scream too much. With these comments in my head, I went back home to be with Johnny who was on his best behavior for a few weeks at most. It didn't take long before we went back to our vicious cycle of violence.

Eventually, he took a break from me and focused on his other woman. He'd been seeing his daughter's mother on and off throughout our relationship, and his family helped him hide it. She was even more conditioned than I was. He'd been with her since she was in middle school and the poor woman was completely under his control. The dynamics between all these families were completely dysfunctional. He and his younger brother were extremely verbally abusive to his mother and even used physical intimidation at times. They would break things and threaten to do things like burn down the house. The sons' relationship was even more dysfunctional and physically violent. I witnessed his brother attempt to stab his father, Johnny fist-fight his dad and younger brother, and them breaking things in the home in fits of rage. It was maddening. And as bad as that was, Johnny often berated me for having a dysfunctional family.

There were countless acts of violence against me, including rape. It got to the point where Johnny controlled what I wore, who I spoke to, how I spoke to people, and who I made eye contact with, even when he wasn't present. The violence and cycles fluctuated with his interest in me, which was determined by the other woman. He sometimes employed other acts of control like withholding food or money to other necessities.

When I had my baby, I became completely consumed by her and the hope of new life. He also let up because he felt less threatened that I would leave him and, at this point, I'd accepted that I would never get away from him. He seemed bigger than life and more powerful than I could ever be. He was so confident in my devotion to my new baby that he made me drive myself home from the hospital when she was born and walk several blocks home carrying her in her car seat along with my bags. When I think back on that now, I realize how cruel it was. At the time, I was just happy to go home alone. During the delivery, Johnny constantly accused me of letting male nurses or doctors see my body. He practically ruined one of the most wonderful experiences of my life, but I still managed to find joy. I can still remember how happy I felt at the hospital with my newborn and not letting her out of my sight for one second. I felt the hope that only true love can evoke.

The next year would be much of the same but the violence was less frequent. In part, it was because he was preoccupied with his other woman, but also because I became extremely submissive leaving little for him to fight about. He enjoyed hurting people in a sadistic, psychopathic way, but he mostly just wanted control.

My relationships with my mother and sister improved during this time. We had more in common than ever since my sister had a baby one month after my daughter was born. Also, I was so overwhelmed by Johnny that I didn't have any space in my mind or heart for anger. I mostly lived in a state of shame and worked extra hard to create the family environment I didn't have growing up. My family—mother, sister, the babies, and I—had our first Thanksgiving celebration ever. I became family oriented and focused all my energy on giving my daughter, Karinna, a real childhood and as much consistency as possible. Johnny created chaos whenever he was around, which made me work extra hard to create a peaceful environment. Luckily, he let me live at my mother's house for months, giving me some alone time with Karinna before he started feeling a loss of control.

I became pregnant again shortly after Karinna's first birthday. I was overwhelmed with sadness to be in the same situation again, especially while he was also having another baby with the other woman. He lost interest in me for most of my second pregnancy, during which time I went to community college. I was so incredibly happy to be back in school. But shortly after one really good semester, Johnny turned his interest toward me again. He began to stalk me at school at all times, and my two-hour commute by bus while pregnant was too much. I ended up dropping out, and I was devastated. It felt as though I'd lost my chance at a new life. By this point, I was already on welfare. Johnny was a criminal. The days of selling jewelry were behind him. He had a new quick money scheme every few months. He couldn't maintain a job even if he wanted to because he spent so much time chasing me and his other woman.

Once I dropped out of school, Johnny left me alone for some time. I think he didn't feel threatened that I might leave him or meet someone else while pregnant and at home with a toddler. I rarely left the house. I spent my days watching Karinna and getting ready for the new baby to arrive. It was nice to be left alone; I enjoyed my Johnny-free time with Karinna, and it made for a much less stressful few months. The baby eventually came, and my sister was my Lamaze partner, allowing me to have a better delivery than the first one.

When Johnny finally made it to the hospital, he ended up being escorted out by security for cursing me out. He didn't like the name I picked and was angry that my sister was my Lamaze partner, so he went on a rant calling me a bitch at the top of his lungs. I retaliated by leaving him off the birth certificate. I would regret that decision later because it made my kids' lives more difficult by constantly having to explain why they had different last names. Once again, I managed to find joy in the experience of becoming a mom for the second time at age twenty-three to my baby girl, Bryanna. It was a lot, but I didn't let myself dwell for very long in the despair of what my life had become at the moment.

The reality eventually set in, and postpartum depression hit me hard for about six months. I cried every single day when I was alone with the girls, which was almost all the time. It was almost debilitating; however, somehow, I still managed to care for them and find quiet moments of pure happiness. It is so crazy how, in all that chaos, my mind managed to escape into a place of pure love and bliss with my girls. Bryanna, nicknamed Bee, was pretty sickly; she developed asthma early on. These were the days when my sister supported me unconditionally. She drove me and Bee to the hospital many nights before I learned to control it. The depression passed, but Bee's asthma issues continued for a few more years. Simultaneously, Johnny would continue to terrorize me. He was in and out of our everyday lives regularly. He was around just enough to keep the fear alive.

Somehow, he convinced me to move into another apartment with him. He needed to isolate me so I would be easier to manipulate, and I hoped that he was being truthful when he said he would give me space if he knew I was in a safe place. He paid all the bills and sometimes bought food when the food stamps ran out, but he started to become angry because I was refusing sex more and more often. He would sometimes resort to violence, but other times he used other tactics. Once, he refused to buy food because I wouldn't have sex with him and I'd run out of food stamps. I only had baby food and one bag of frozen french fries in the house. I was still breast-feeding Bee, and Kari was on baby food. I lived off of those fries for a week by baking them in the oven because I didn't even have oil. These types of games became the new manipulation tactics as the violence became less frequent but more extreme.

There was one night when Kari had been sick with the stomach flu. I'd been refusing sex for weeks, and the food deprivation just wasn't as effective once I adjusted and learned to avoid it. He came into the apartment in the early morning hours while the girls and I were sleeping. He was talking to me while I slept, and I guess I was responding in a half-conscious state. According to what he told me, he whispered in my ear asking me if I loved him, and my response was "let me see your face". He violently shook me and abruptly woke me up. I was exhausted and overwhelmed with confusion. He ordered me to go to the living room. I knew he was angry by his demeanor but had no idea why.

Our apartment had no furniture except a TV on the floor of the living room, and a mattress in the bedroom with a toddler bed and a crib. The kitchen had a small table with a few chairs and basic appliances. Still, this apartment was much better than the place I grew up in. He told me to sit, so I sat on the floor with my legs crossed, and he sat directly in front of me while the girls slept in the other room.

Without warning, he punched me in the face harder than I'd ever been hit before. I clearly remember the way my head bounced back and hit the wall behind me, and I felt my brain shake. I experienced the distorted feeling I often felt when he hit me directly in my face and nose. It was as though my nose had been pushed into my brain and the very unique taste of metal in my mouth that accompanied the pain. I started to cry, but he immediately ordered me to stop crying and answer his questions. He interrogated me for what seemed like hours about my dream and whose face I needed to see. I felt like I was still dreaming; it was so incredibly insane that he expected answers.

I could feel warm blood streaming down my face. I wasn't sure where it was coming from since my entire head ached. I felt as though I'd been hit by a ton of bricks and my entire face was swelling. As I sat, looking at him in the eyes at all times because if my stare strayed, he would accuse me of lying, I noticed the white walls were covered with streaks and splashes of blood. I started to get lightheaded, so I mustered up the courage to ask him to go to the bathroom. When I looked in the mirror, I fainted. When I came to, I looked at my face again. I could see my cheekbone through the hole he'd made in my face. I had skin hanging, and I was bleeding profusely. When I told him I needed stitches, he argued that I just needed a Band-Aid. I attempted the Band-Aid, but it fell off over and over again as it became saturated with blood. Finally, after several hours of back and forth, he agreed to drop me off at the emergency room. He gave me specific instructions when he dropped me off, ordering me not to talk to anyone and to tell them I already spoke to the police if they asked what happened. He left me with a final threat: Don't forget, I have your precious girls.

When I arrived, I waited several hours for a plastic surgeon due to the location of the injury; it was right below my left eye. By this point, my entire face was distorted. I looked hideous. While I waited, a nurse came to my bed to tell me that my brother was on the phone. I knew that it couldn't be my brother since he was estranged from the family. When I picked up, Johnny reminded me again that he had the girls and would hurt them if necessary. I reassured him that I wouldn't tell. He went on to say that he would make it up to me, that we just needed a vacation because I'd been too difficult lately, and how my refusal to have sex made him insecure. He told me that we would go to Canada for a few weeks. He also reminded me a few more times that he had the girls and that I would never see them again if I told anyone what happened or called the police. I agreed to do whatever he wanted after I got treated.

The plastic surgeon spent hours stitching up my face. He gave me forty stitches over several layers to minimize the scarring. He asked me why it took me so long to get help. I told him that I didn't have a ride. The reality is, I was happy to have someone validate my reaction. Johnny repeatedly told me that I was exaggerating and didn't need medical attention. When the surgeon finished, I called Johnny who picked me up with the girls in the car. I was so relieved to see the girls again after all his threats that I didn't care what was wrong with my face.

The next few weeks were brutal. My face was completed distorted. This time, I didn't just look bad, I actually felt terrible. The headaches were incapacitating but I still had to take care of my girls. After a few days, I worked up the courage to call my cousin. She is Karinna's godmother and Johnny liked her. I had a dress that belonged to her daughter, so I used it as my excuse to call her and get her to come to my house without directly inviting her. I casually said that I had it ready whenever she wanted to pick it up. Later, she told me that she could tell by my voice that I was asking for help.

She lost her mind when she saw my face. She cried hysterically. She was horrified and could not believe what I was telling her. She came into the apartment and saw the blood splatters on the walls and my wound once I removed the gauze. It was like something out of a movie. She told me to get some clothes and jump in the car with my girls to get away. She took me to my aunt's house where my cousins, mother, and sister gathered to come up with a plan. At this point, my fear of Johnny was illogical. I was convinced he could hear everything I said and even read my mind. Later, I would learn that I had PTSD. I experienced panic attacks, couldn't sleep, and walked around in a fog in complete disassociation from reality. I was afraid and confused all the time.

I found a shelter that would take me and my girls; Kari was two years and Bee was six months old at this point. A van picked us up that evening and took us to an undisclosed location. The shelter was for women and children who were the victims of domestic violence. When I got there, with minimal items, I was signed in and given a room. The girls and I had a bed and shared a shower with others. It was a pretty rundown place full of women who'd lived rough lives including drug use, prostitution, and homelessness. It was definitely not a place for small children, but it was safer than our home. I remember being told that I needed to keep their things close and that the refrigerator had a lock. I was told I could ask to have someone open it if I needed milk for the girls. Luckily, I was still breastfeeding Bee. It was a surreal experience.

After a few days with a few scares and uncomfortable interactions with some of the other women and kids at the place, I decided that this environment wasn't helping me. I called my cousin, who somehow convinced them to give her the address, and she came to pick us up. She let us stay at her house for three months, which seemed like the longest three months ever. I started therapy for my panic attacks but continued to experience severe PTSD. My cousin, her husband, and other members of my family worked hard to help me recover—but the truth is that I was too lost in the darkness of my mind and Johnny's influence. I had lost all concept of what real life was like and what independence looked like. I'd had every aspect of my life controlled for so long that I was afraid to just live.

After my cousin's, I went to stay at my sister's house, which was complete chaos. My sister's life was just as unhinged as mine but in different ways. After staying at her house for a few days, Johnny showed up at her door. I was alone with the kids while my sister was at work. I guess Johnny had been watching the house and showed up when everyone left. When I opened the door, he opened his jacket to show me the gun he had in the waistband of his pants. He reminded me of all the times I'd called the cops and they either hadn't come for hours or never showed up at all. He told me to get in the car with the girls because he had made plans for us. I grabbed my bag and the girls, and got into his car, no questions asked. Once in the car, he told me he forgave me for leaving him all that time and said he was sorry for what he did.

We drove to an airport, he bought tickets, and we took a flight to Puerto Rico that same evening. All I had was my diaper bag with diapers and a change of clothes for the girls. When we landed in Puerto Rico hours later, he rented a car and got us a room in some strange looking motel. I remember washing the girls' clothes by hand and holding the girls in the shower as I washed them. It didn't feel real. I couldn't accept that this was my life. The only way I could survive was by numbing every part of my person; mind, heart, and body. I fully immersed myself in taking care of the girls. I was at Johnny's mercy more than ever, but I still hadn't reached my limit, so I kept trying. I had not reached the moment when I'd be willing to do anything to get away from this man. Life with him was still less painful than life with my family and, most of all, the past I was trying so hard to forget.

The next three months in Puerto Rico were full of loneliness and a constant state of alertness. Johnny had a few cousins that helped us find a house to rent where I spent endless hours alone with the girls. We had two mattresses, a stove, minimal cooking appliances, and basic things like a few changes of clothes. Bee, who was about nine months, became sick with an intestinal infection from the water. Johnny agreed to let me come back to New Jersey to get her the care she needed. We'd find out a few weeks later that she also had a skin infection that we'd all get.

When we returned to New Jersey, I had nowhere to go since my mother had given up her apartment to live with my grandmother. We ended up sleeping on Johnny's mother's living room floor while he figured out his next move. His plans typically consisted of a way to get me far from my family—I also wanted to be away from them, but for different reasons. He wanted more control, and I wanted to heal from the abuse.

Weeks later, he cooked up his next plan; we would move to California where we would have a fresh start. He convinced me that he and I would drive there alone, set up the new apartment, and then bring the girls by plane. I left the girls with my mother and drove with him for a week. By this time, I was close to twenty-four years old and living a life of abuse, fear, and trauma. I often found myself at the extremes of sex filled with desperate attempts at a real connection or beatings that ended with death threats. Whatever happened between those extremes happened in a fog of emotionless movements.

Johnny, the girls, and I lived in Anaheim, California, for three months. I was in a constant state of fear. The abuse escalated again because I was pretending less and less. I stopped acting like everything was fine all the time and that I was happy despite his abusive behavior. I was getting closer and closer to my limit, the place where I stopped giving a fuck. He became more sexually abusive since I stopped fighting him off because it was just us. I was so isolated and vulnerable. I slept with the girls every night on the floor in the bedroom, and he'd come to get me once they were sleeping. I'd pretend to be asleep, and he'd whisper threats in my ear some nights until I gave in, other nights he'd just leave. The threats became more graphic and detailed.

Finally, he left for some type of business dealing for an extended period of time. He left me the car and $100 with strict instructions to not call my family while he was gone. The same day he left, I put the girls, who were one and two, into a stroller and walked to a mall about forty-five minutes away to use a pay phone. I called my mother collect and told her I needed help. The violence and threats were escalating, and I knew he was going to kill me.

My mother bought plane tickets for me and Karinna. Bee was still young enough to sit on my lap. Next, I called and arranged for a cab to pick us up first thing the next morning. I packed a diaper bag with traveling essentials and took Bee's car seat and left everything else we had behind for the fourth time. I remember running through the airport with this immense pit in my stomach expecting him to appear at any moment. We made our way onto the plane and began our six-hour flight home. When we finally arrived at Newark Airport, my sister and our friend Lori picked us up from the airport, and I felt safe for the first time in years.

I went to stay at my grandmother's house, and it didn't take Johnny long to find me. Initially, he was completely out of control per usual—until he found out I was pregnant again. I was devastated once again. It seemed as though I would never get out, and I tried desperately to accept that this is what my life was and would always be: an abusive partner, welfare, more kids, and no stability or peace for the rest of our lives. He was thrilled because he knew it would be impossible for me to leave him or start a new life.

The next ten months flew by. I slept on my grandmother's pullout couch with my mom and the girls while my belly got bigger and bigger. At the end of my pregnancy, both my mother and Johnny bought houses. My mom bought a house a town over from Paterson, where we were living with my grandmother, and Johnny bought a house a few towns over. I moved into my mother's basement in July of 1998, and I was due to give birth in August. Johnny wanted me to move into the house he bought, but he didn't push too hard because as long as I was inundated with babies, he was winning. Sebastian was born on August 10, 1998, at a nearby hospital. Johnny gleamed with pride at having a son and immediately became impatient. He wanted me to come live with him at all costs. I was able to buy myself a few weeks with the excuse of having a newborn and having just given birth, but Johnny didn't care and started to push harder and harder.

Two weeks into my post-pregnancy recovery, I was home alone with the three kids when I heard knocking on the back door. I opened it to find him standing there. I told him that he couldn't come in because my mother didn't want him in the house. I'd told him that before, but clearly, he didn't care. He pushed the door open and started slapping me for not letting him in. I was holding two-week-old Sebastian, and Karinna and Bryanna came running in startled by his yelling and my crying. I told the girls to go hide, and Karinna grabbed Bryanna's hand and they ran downstairs together. Johnny continued to hit me and tried to take Sebastian from me. I screamed and cried, continually trying to protect my newborn.

This went on for a pretty long time until suddenly, there was a knock on the door followed by a male voice saying, "Totowa police". Johnny immediately ordered me to shut up and to tell the cops everything was fine. I opened the door after several knocks and told the officer that I didn't want Johnny there and that he'd hurt me. He called Johnny out and told him that he should go for a walk and not come back. Johnny, of course, attempted to charm him, but the cop just insisted he leave for now. He could clearly see I was distressed. It didn't matter what the cop did, Johnny was gone for the moment.

I immediately went looking for the girls and found them hiding in a closet. I got them ready and called my sister asking her to please come get me. I was deathly afraid to be in the house alone now. My sister picked me up in her little blue escort, and we drove to my mom's salon in Paterson. While we were parking the car at metered parking on the street, Johnny pulled up in his huge Lexus truck and ran into my sister's car with us all in it. He hit the driver's side door where I was sitting. The door was completely pushed in and the car had been moved several feet onto the sidewalk. Johnny got out of his car and walked up to my window to get me out. Fortunately, the door wouldn't open, and when he reached in to get me, I fought him off. When he noticed people were starting to gather to see what was happening, he jumped into his car and drove off. I looked around at my three kids and my sister all in the smashed car with me, and I decided at that moment that it was over.

I took the kids into my mother's salon and started to put a plan together. I went to a notary who drafted and notarized a letter giving my mother custody of my kids in my death. I then went to the police station to discuss my issues in detail with an officer. As per usual, the cops didn't care about my personal struggles and weren't interested until I started sharing information about Johnny's crimes. The cop looked him up using the information I provided and found that Johnny was on the FBI's most wanted list. He gave me a phone number to call, which I did as soon as I got home. Once I shared my information, they asked me to come in for further investigation. At the FBI office, I was escorted into a conference room where I identified him from an array of photos. We worked on a plan that would be the craziest and most dangerous thing I'd done up to that point of my life—and maybe even until now.

At the FBI headquarters, I explained to a group of agents what'd happened and gave them all of the information I knew regarding his multiple identities, dealings, and crimes. I also offered to help catch him. The entire time I was in the building, my heart was in my throat. First, a couple of agents went with me to my grandmother's house where I knew he would try to contact me. When he called, the agents listened and coaxed me through the conversation. He was demanding to see the kids. I told him that I would meet him, but that I would take a cab since my sister's car was damaged from the crash. We agreed to meet at a train commuter parking lot about twenty minutes from my grandmother's house in Paterson. The FBI agent had explained that we couldn't set up a meeting in a busy place like the mall because it would put too many bystanders in danger. One of the FBI agents escorted me to get a cab, and he drove in the cab driver's place. Five unmarked police cars were supposed to be hiding nearby as well.

I had left all three kids at my mom's salon with the notarized letter in case anything went wrong. I cannot find the words to explain the state my body was in as we drove up to the lot, parked, and waited. I felt every muscle and nerve in my body twitch while the blood pumped through my veins at an unbelievable speed. All I could hear was my heart pounding while I could barely breathe. I felt as though my body would give out on me any minute. It was a similar feeling to the fear I felt during that first beating five years earlier in the ShopRite parking lot. The agent reminded me several times that as soon as I saw Johnny, I had to describe his clothes and what he looked like so they could have a description on record to arrest him. The agent had a shotgun in the front that I could see from the backseat.

Suddenly, I saw Johnny walking toward the cab in full stride. I quickly described his beige cargo shorts, white and blue golf shirt, and sneakers, followed by a quick description of his dark hair, fair skin, and dark brown eyes. He got to the cab in what seemed like seconds, and attempted to open my door in the back, but it was locked. I never made eye contact as he banged on the window telling me to open the door. He immediately knew something was wrong. It wasn't like me to ignore his direct commands. He looked in the front window and saw the agent with the shotgun next to him. Johnny started cursing at me, shouting "Bitch what did you do?" over and over again. Then, a bunch of cars sped into the lot and one pinned him against the cab. I never looked at him, but I could hear the cop say, "You like hitting women," followed by what sounded like punches. I sat, frozen, holding my breath until the agent driving the cab pulled out of the lot onto the street. It was by far the craziest thing I'd ever experienced.

I was still in a state of shock when later that evening my mother's home phone rang. When I answered, it was Johnny calling from jail threatening me. Everything had happened so fast that I hadn't even really had time to process it. Had it really only been this morning that he'd shown up banging on the door and now he's calling me from jail? Even through this immense relief that I felt at finally being away from him, that fear that he could continue to hurt me was still there.

For years after, Johnny and his family made my life miserable fighting for visitations with the kids, custody, and even calling Child Protective Services on me. Johnny was sentenced to five years for aggravated assault with a deadly weapon, but he was out in eighteen months. He fought me in court a little but ultimately decided to leave me alone, and I opted to pass on child support to cut all ties. The PTSD persisted for many years. I would imagine seeing him all the time. I had nightmares and occasional panic attacks. The nightmares persisted for years during every high stress period in my life.

The day Johnny went to prison was life-altering for me. I found an internal strength I'd lost years prior. I'd spent so much time feeling unsafe and afraid that I didn't remember what fighting back felt like. It was amazing. I felt like I had found a part of me I'd lost during my journey. I felt fearless. If I could beat Johnny, I could do anything. He was by far the most violent, unpredictable, and obsessive person I'd ever met.

There was also a part of me that was afraid to start this new chapter where I was off on my own making all the decisions about my kids. Suddenly, it was all me. I had the full burden of raising three kids on my own, protecting them from my past and my family, and being the only breadwinner. It felt all consuming; however, I refused to dwell on it for too long. I felt the enormous weight every day, but I didn't allow myself the luxury of self-pity or fear. All I allowed myself to absorb was the freedom and new lease on life. I had found a new sense of gratitude. I was grateful for a second shot at life with a clear purpose of getting these kids out of poverty and creating a space away from my family. It's interesting to reflect on it now. I didn't know what generational trauma was, I didn't know what boundaries within relationships were, I didn't know the difference between abuse or love yet—I just knew that I wanted my kids to have a different life.

I also went through withdrawal from Johnny. There were many lonely nights when I craved love and affection. I was twenty-five years old and had already experienced a lifetime of pain with little experience of what real love felt like. Still, the chemical addiction of the ups and downs of the abusive cycle were like withdrawal from drugs. I craved the feeling of being chosen, loved, and seen, even if it was followed by extreme abuse. The commitment to giving my kids a better life and creating a life away from my family was stronger than the addiction so I rode it out until I felt sober.

Once Sandi and I worked through this very obvious trauma, we started to dig much deeper; the parts of my life that made me vulnerable to abusers like Johnny and Kevin. What happened to me growing up had created a landscape in my mind for abusers to thrive in—and so we moved on to my childhood.

### REFLECTIONS FROM RECOVERY
- Physical and sexual violence are about power and control not sex or love.
- Victims of abuse can become victims, empaths, or abusers. All abusers are victims of abuse who never healed and can't deal with the process of self-reflection. Our traumas are not our fault—still, our recovery is our responsibility. Abusers are responsible for their path and their behavior regardless of their childhood pain.
- Familial patterns are ingrained in us and show up in our closest relationships. They are created during our childhood and show up out in our romantic relationships where we replay them in an unconscious attempt to change the outcome of our past experiences. We minimize the impact of childhood trauma in our adult lives because it is easier than it is to acknowledge it and feel it.
- Freeze and faun are common responses to violence or a threatening environment. Most people imagine that fight or flight are the only logical responses. Dissociation was my way of surviving constant violent episodes.
- It's hard to make progress in therapy while in an abusive relationship; however, it will help to identify the patterns, validate the experiences, and develop positive coping mechanisms.

### RECOMMENDED RESOURCES AND INFORMATION
**Recognizing signs of abuse:**
- Warning Signs of an Abusive Relationship - New Hope, Inc. (new-hope.org): https://www.new-hope.org/warning-signs-of-an-abusive-relationship/

- 25 Signs You're in an Abusive Relationship (choosingtherapy.com): https://www.choosingtherapy.com/abusive-relationship/
- Abusive Relationships: 6 Signs To Look For (webmd.com): https://www.webmd.com/sex-relationships/signs-abusive-relationship

## Chapter 4 - Where It All Began

I was born in San Jose, Costa Rica, in July of 1973 to Anabelle and Alejandro. They were both twenty-eight years old and already had a seven-year-old daughter and ten-year-old son. We were a middle-class family. My dad worked outside the home, and my mom stayed at home full time. I was the unplanned child, and I really don't know if they hesitated to have me or not. Back in those days, the lifestyle in Costa Rica was pretty laid back for my family; however, it was a lot of work. My mother washed clothes by hand and spent all day doing housework while caring for every one of the kids' needs. My father was gone all day, and when he arrived at night, he expected to be fully catered to. It was exactly what society deemed an acceptable household in the '70s. My life seemed secure and stable—but it really wasn't.

I have very few memories of my early childhood; however, the few memories I do have are vivid. I remember my father physically abusing my mother. I can picture walking into our large kitchen to a violent scene that has always lived with me. My dad was holding my mother over our red clay double kitchen sink. He was hitting her while choking her as she screamed and begged him to stop. Although I was about five years old at the time, this event was extremely impactful and has become a permanent fixture in my mind. That particular incident was the one that made the biggest impression on me, but it was by no means an isolated incident. It was one of many acts of violence in our otherwise great life. My father was particularly violent with my older brother, who I have very few only vague memories of. He was also extremely controlling over my teenage sister, and his jealousy over my mother was violence-ridden and illogical. I was spared as I was too young to be trouble or invoke his need to control others.

The conflict between my parents seemed to get worse as my father's many affairs became more of an issue for my mother. For my mother, violence was acceptable, but cheating crossed the line. However, my dad did his fair share of blaming my mother for the troubles in their marriage. I distinctly remember one occasion when they were arguing over accusations he was making of her cheating with our neighbor's brother. He asked me if I thought she flirted with the neighbor—which, in retrospect, seems odd to ask a child. I recall wanting to gain my father's approval and agreeing to his unfounded accusations. I have carried the guilt associated with that night through my entire adult life, often wondering if my mother was beaten as a result of my exaggerations.

My father's affection was like no other I've ever known; his kisses and hugs always seemed to fill my heart in such an intense way. He always made me feel so special and loved when he paid attention to me. It was the reason I sold out my mother that night, for his approval and love. In fact, he still caused these feelings of love and approval well into adulthood on the few occasions I saw him. I've been searching for that type of love all my life.

I have two specific memories of my dad and I spending time alone. There was one glorious day at the beach and one occasion at my favorite pool. In Costa Rica, access to the beach or pool is common due to the tropical weather all year round. It wasn't an incredibly special outing; however, in my mind, it was wonderful. I recall the quiet ride home while I mostly slept after a few hours under the sun and in the water. To this day, the beach and swimming are among my favorite activities. The best part of the outing was my dad carrying me into the house while I pretended to sleep. I remember my dad as a loud, charming, and attractive man. He is the most physically affectionate person I've ever known. His love was like a warm blanket on a cold day. It covered all of me, and I wanted it to. His attention filled me with pride, as if I was someone special. He made me feel like I was the only person in the room or the only person he could love. However, most of the time, he was not around, which often left me feeling empty.

I have no memory of any conversations regarding my parents' separation or divorce. I remember shopping in town with my mother on one occasion and seeing my father with another woman—his mistress. My mom rushed me along onto a bus to avoid confronting him in front of me. They'd been married for eighteen years, since she was seventeen years old, and she'd had enough. She was in her mid-thirties, and she'd dedicated her life to her kids and husband with little-to-no room for her to ever be her own person. The many years of violence, uncontrollable jealousy, and infidelity were too much for her to take any longer.

Suddenly, my dad was gone, and I was still at home with just my mother and sister. My brother had already left; he'd been sent to America by my parents at some point when I was around six. I have no recollection of my father or my brother saying goodbye, packing, or walking out. My memory jumps from a few vague memories of my father in the house, violence, and then he was gone.

After the separation, my mom, who had been a dedicated homemaker and mother, was now preoccupied with self-discovery. She prided herself on being likable and attractive. She loved being the go-to person for all her friends and acquaintances for love and sex advice. She talked about it openly as if it was a special gift. It was like she had the high school popularity syndrome at thirty-five. She was loved by all, which left her too busy for me unless I was the center of attention.

I was one of the more popular girls in our little neighborhood because I was deemed especially attractive. I got attention regularly for my looks and my over-achievement in school. I took great pride in being independent at an early age; by kindergarten, I'd declared I didn't need help with school. She loved that because it took away the burden she experienced with my siblings. My mother was reclaiming the youth she never had, making it impossible for me to feel safe or stable.

After many years of my father's control and abuse, my mother and sister were finally able to breathe. They began to party together and started acting more like sisters. My mom became the "cool mom", and my house became the party house. Young people were constantly coming over to hang out, have parties, and engage in activities that I shouldn't have been exposed to at such a young age.

We didn't have any family that was close enough to create a buffer or safety net for me. My sister was a teenager, so she was thrilled to see the authority figure leave the house, but I still needed parental attention and guidance. It was scary for me to suddenly go from having this dedicated parent who gave me stability to suddenly feeling more like I had another sister. I only knew that my mother was no longer the mother I once knew and the dad who made me feel incredible joy when he was around was gone.

One of my most vivid memories of this time is of my mother locked in her bedroom with an eighteen-year-old who my sister had dated briefly. I recall seeing that the light was off in the room and the door was locked. I knocked insensately because I knew that they were engaging in something that made me uncomfortable. My stomach was in knots as I knocked on the door over and over. My mother repeatedly told me to stop. I kept asking what they were doing, and she insisted they were looking at photo albums and they'd be out shortly—but I knew it wasn't true.

Not long after, a woman I didn't know moved into the house for a few months. She was the mistress of a Colombian drug dealer who needed a place to stay until he got out of jail, so she rented my brother's bedroom. She made such an impression on me; she was like no other woman I'd ever seen before. She dressed in fancy clothes, had a lot of expensive-looking jewelry, and felt comfortable walking around in her beautiful lace undergarments. She was also incredibly beautiful, and confidence oozed out of her. She seemed so confident in her body, her ability to communicate, and her life choices. She was completely unapologetic and flaunted all that she was. I was in awe in her presence. I can still remember sitting at the end of her bed watching her get ready to go dancing as she put her makeup on and walked around in her lace bra and underwear.

Needless to say, it was a lot for me at six years old. There was a lot of alcohol, drug, and sex talk when she was around—and I listened to every word and absorbed it all. I became very aware of sexuality. I was sensitive to my mother's many conversations with her peers and younger people about sex or sexuality. I was around many young people who were in the prime of their puberty, and it all had its effect on my impressionable young mind.

In my mother's and sister's efforts to help me be popular, our house also became a place where many young kids would hang out. My sister would arrange make-believe beauty contests where I was always the winner regardless of who played or judged. I learned quickly, although I am pretty sure I already knew, how to become the center of attention and the life of the party. I learned that my physical appearance and outgoing personality were highly valued by others—and that my intelligence was not valued in the same way.

And then suddenly, once again, everything changed. I don't remember packing, discussions, or the decision to move. I only remember being at the Miami airport with my mother and sister making our way to America. I don't know what my expectations could have possibly been for moving to a new country at only eight years old. I just remember a sad feeling that ties back to my father. I have a vague memory of watching my father as we walked away from him at the airport in Costa Rica. The tears ran down my face and my gut hurt, but there was no time for emotions. We needed to move on and just let it go, and so I did. The pain never went away.

Our first bed in America was on the floor of the dining room in my grandmother's third-floor apartment. She had a small one-bedroom apartment with a hallway that ran through every room making privacy impossible. It seemed like an okay neighborhood in Paterson, NJ. It was a place full of people from different countries—a concept that was difficult for me to grasp at first. I came from a small town in Costa Rica where most people were native. This place was so different from what I knew. Everything was intimidating—from the languages to the buildings, to what seemed to me like fancy apartments with such an abundance of food. My grandmother worked hard to make me feel loved by her, and she did a hell of a job. To this day, I still feel her love.

My first Christmas in the US was amazing. My grandmother, step-grandfather, aunt, brother, and four cousins made it absolutely wonderful. It was a very warm, welcoming feeling. It was the strength of family—of stability and safety. My mother seemed to suddenly become grounded again. She began to work, and although that was super difficult for me because I was used to being home with her, it was better than the partying. My brother and I began building a new relationship, and he became my hero.

We lived with my grandmother for about six months until we moved into our own apartment across the street. It was a building that had partially burned down; it seemed nice with new paint. I was ecstatic to not have to sleep on the floor in the middle of my grandmother's dining room anymore. We had actual bedrooms; although, I would continue to sleep with my mother for about a year. The apartment turned out to be pretty crappy once we moved in, full of rodents, roaches, and no air conditioning. Nowhere close to the American dream.

When we initially moved into this inner-city neighborhood, it was tolerable; however, after one summer, it changed drastically—a direct result of the crack epidemic. The street was once called Little Italy because it was heavily populated by Italians and little coffee shops that were fronts for illegal gambling. We lived close to the projects and other low-income housing similar to our apartment building. It was predominately minorities besides the Italians.

I didn't really know how poor we were until I became an adult. I thought all people in the US lived the same way we did. We didn't go on vacation, own a car, or do much of anything other than work, go to school, or watch TV. In retrospect, it was a pretty sad life; although, not different than many of my neighbors, but I do think our financial situation was tighter than some.

I was still fairly innocent at this point in my life, although I'd already experienced some trauma. I remember spending endless hours lost in games that took me far away from my reality. I would play with my barbies on the roof outside my window in between the buildings. I was with my grandmother on the weekends while my mother worked seven days a week. As I was the youngest of all of the grandkids by at least six years, I spent most of my time playing alone. My siblings were in their late teens, which made the prospect of hanging out with me not very attractive. I spent my summers looking out the window at night when it was too hot to sleep, watching other kids in the neighborhood walk around and play, enjoying the peace of a quiet street in a calm neighborhood.

As the crack epidemic got worse, so did my street. I watched as more and more sex workers made the corner outside my house their working spot. Drugs, drug dealers, and violence ran rampant. On my way to school and on the playground, I would step over condoms on the ground while dodging the men attempting to pick me up for sex work. It became a much tougher place to live. It was a weird transition; I wanted to hold on to my innocence, but it was almost impossible. The city had built a park with a tall round fountain where we played in the water in the summer, but within years, that same fountain became a spot for people to sell drugs, get high, and then wash up.

The neighborhood continued to change through the '80s as other drugs like meth hit the streets. Prostitution was becoming much more common affecting everyone in the area. I saw girls from the neighborhood become prostitutes to support their drug habits. The struggles of the community became evident to me as I watched out my window each night. It became more and more of a struggle to be a kid in that environment. A task as simple as walking down the street to the store became dreadful and challenging. There was a strip club on my block that I had to pass on the way to get my brother's cigarettes or even my candy. The level of harassment I experienced from the men going in and out was intolerable. However, like most women, I learned to laugh it off or curse out the men who became aggressive when I ignored them—except I was still only a child.

I was going to Public School No. 2 in our neighborhood, which was not a forgiving place. The school was underfunded and incredibly scary for me because it was way bigger than any school I'd ever been in, I didn't speak English, and I was in the midst of a major culture shock. I annoyed my teachers and classmates because of my constant confusion and inability to understand what was happening. I was always asking questions or just plain lost. It was frustrating for all but mostly anxiety-provoking for me. I quickly became a victim of bullying, my grades dropped, and I was involved in a bunch of fights with bigger and older girls. I was extremely unhappy.

Third grade started to look up since I had learned English and made a few friends. Fourth grade was soured by a male teacher who put his hands on my knees and rubbed my thighs. He would tell me to sit next to him during our reading time so he would have easy access to me. I can't start to explain how this violation made me feel. My cousin, who was in high school, wrote a letter regarding his behavior, and suddenly, he was transferred to another school. It was the one and only time a family member handled a situation like this appropriately, which made me feel empowered for a little while.

While I was learning to cope with all the changes in our neighborhood and issues at school, my mother was going through her own drama constantly. My sister was wilding out with my cousins who were in her age group. They partied, got in trouble constantly, and caused a lot of conflict between my mother and my aunt. My brother was full of his own demons ranging from pent-up rage to drug use. But my mother was still determined to live the life she missed out on during her youth. She started partying here and, unfortunately, I often ended up at these parties with her, making me a prime candidate for dangerous situations.

There is one incident that sticks out in my mind because of all the shame it caused me. The only person I have ever shared the details of this incident with is Sandi. It was some type of house party like many of the others we'd been attending. The party included adults, alcohol, music, and some kids. As in many other parties, the kids were segregated to a separate room to give the adults guilt-free partying space. However, the kids' ages ranged from as young as me, nine, to as old as eighteen. As the night passed, the older kids engaged in conversation and eventually wanted to play more mature games like spin the bottle. I, of course, swore I was grown, so I played along with the teenagers. Eventually, I ended up making out with the eighteen-year-old there and later on the porch after he told me that he'd joined the military and would be leaving the following week. The making out advanced quickly into full-on groping and, eventually, he put his hand in my underwear and sexually molested me. I went home that night full of mixed emotions that I didn't know how to process.

I didn't understand that I'd been molested by an adult man at the age of nine. I operated under the impression that it was my decision to engage in the sexual act. Some of the other kids were telling me how lucky I was that he'd picked me. I felt special and grown up—not used or taken advantage of. Days passed, during which I wallowed in my shame and attempted to romanticize the event to make myself feel better. I convinced myself that I had been in full control, the guy genuinely liked me, and I consented—all falsehoods meant to give me back my dignity.

About a week later, without any warning, my mother called me to confront me about the events of that night. I was completely taken off guard. When she asked me if it was true that I made out with the guy and "let" him touch me, I denied it emphatically, as if my life depended on it, because it felt as though it did. Her questions were more like accusations, full of blame and disgust. I took on the full responsibility of that evening just like I'd done in the past and would continue to for the rest of my life, not understanding that I was a child and he was an adult. I carried that shame in my heart and mind until Sandi opened the doors to the place in my mind where all my shame, guilt, and self-loathing lay.

Shortly after, I was transferred to a Catholic private school within walking distance of my house. I'd finish the fifth, sixth, and eighth grades at this school; I skipped seventh grade as a result of extremely high state test scores. During my time there, I was often in trouble for poor behavior. As with most private schools, it was full of secrets. There were a few boys in the school who, like most middle school boys, were sex crazy. They would often lift up the girls' skirts, including mine. Many of them did even worse things; for example, I remember running into two brothers, the worst of the bunch, in the stairwell alone. They grabbed my breasts and ass and lifted my skirt to try to grab my vagina. They were more aggressive than most. In retrospect, the crazy part isn't what they did but how the school handled it. I wasn't the only one these things happened to, but if any girl reported them to the school administration, she was treated as the aggressor. Her parents were called to be informed of the incident, which wasn't just humiliating but it victimized us all over again. It was safer to avoid them at all costs and not report any incidents.

That school caused me even more pain, especially by reinforcing my feelings of unworthiness and shame. The entire Catholic ideology is based on shame and guilt—just like my family experience. I was heavily tied to the teachings of the church during my youth and during my time with Johnny. Catholicism also heavily reinforced the idea of forgiveness no matter what and sacrificing yourself for others, which would also feed into my narrative of abuse. The administration and staff all lived up to that same motto of shaming kids for normal kid behavior to hide their own shame.

When I reported the incident in the stairwell, my mother and grandmother were called into the school to discuss my actions. When my grandmother questioned how the incident had been handled, the monsignor of the church affiliated with the school told my grandmother I was a whore and implied that I was asking for it. Needless to say, at the age of twelve, hearing those words coming out of my grandmother's mouth when she repeated them to me was extremely painful and demoralizing. I was so angry and felt so worthless. I was carrying way too many burdens and was in so much pain for such a young woman. My grandmother had been a loyal parishioner for over twenty years, often donating money, but she stopped going after this ordeal—she was my only supporter. Years later, we would find out that the monsignor had been molesting those brothers for years, and he went to a facility for sex offenders. I will say that it made me feel validated to know that he was the fucked-up person, not me. I was just a kid, and so were those boys. Meanwhile, I had ongoing battles at home.

My mom remarried when I was around ten to a guy who was about eighteen years younger than her, which made him only a year or two older than my brother. It was difficult to see him as a parental figure or role model; he was a kid. In fact, my siblings and I had mixed feelings about him and the role he would play in our family. Nonetheless, he moved in and gave my mother the second chance she desperately needed while creating an uncomfortable household environment for me and my siblings. I rebelled in every which way I could. We argued a lot as he showed so much hostility toward me, and I refused to acknowledge his authority over me. Eventually, in order to create some space between me and my stepfather, I moved into my aunt's house, which became a safe place for me at the time.

After about a year, I moved back in. I had zero privacy since my bed was in the corner of the living room, and at eleven years old, I had zero space to just be a kid. All of a sudden, my stepfather started to express an interest in me in a way that was confusing to me. He began to tell me that he was in love with me. He would tell me that he married my mother because he wanted to be close to me and have a romantic relationship with me. It started gradually with small gestures over many months that later turned into his confession of love. He eventually told me that he wanted to have sex with me. Since I didn't have any privacy or space in the house, he was always creeping nearby. The worst times were when we were home alone in the mornings after my mother left to work. He would caress my face or hair while I was getting ready for school. I told my sister and brother, but their advice was that I avoid him and not tell my mother. This continued for years, although he never went beyond holding my hand. The anxiety and fear he caused during my formative pre-teen years were incredibly traumatic. The trauma from this experience influenced the way I'd see men and myself for the rest of my life. This was just the beginning of the severe emotional abuse that I suffered at home.

Then, my brother's then-girlfriend of many years told my grandmother about my stepfather. I am not sure why she told her, but she definitely didn't do it to protect me. However, it shined a light on the gruesome secret I'd been carrying for years. With the help of my siblings, I'd been protecting my stepfather's sins for years as though they were my sins. It caused me great shame because everyone acted as though I did something wrong, which reinforced his narrative. He consistently told me it was my fault that he loved me and wanted to marry me; a very confusing message for a kid that age.

Ultimately, my grandmother told my mother who confronted me and him as though we'd been keeping a secret together. I told her the truth, even though I was so young and really intimated by the entire situation. He initially denied it, but I stood my ground. He eventually admitted it; however, his version of the truth had an interesting twist. He told my mother that his behavior was his way of coping with my poor behavior. He was frustrated with my rebellious behavior and used sexual abuse to punish me for being a bratty kid. Not only was it a crazy explanation, but it taught me at thirteen years old that sex could be used as a weapon. It messed me up on so many levels, but mostly in that my mother gave him a second chance. After all those years of abuse, he didn't have to deal with any repercussions whatsoever. It was pretty devastating. Especially considering my stepfather only managed to make it through another year before my mother met another man and decided to leave him. I remember helping her get him out so she could bring her new boyfriend to the house. The level of resentment I felt toward my mother was more than I could understand at that age. It was by far the worse betrayal I'd experienced at my mother's hand up to that point, but it would get worse later.

While I was dealing with the psychological abuse from my stepfather, I was surrounded by two other hugely dysfunctional relationships in the house. Living in my mother's house with me were with my mother, stepfather, brother, sister, sister's husband, and baby nephew. It was full of anxiety, constant drama, and chaos, particularly for me as the youngest sibling. It was not a safe place for a kid to grow up.

My sister had gotten married to a young guy who was abusive and addicted to drugs. My sister's was the second relationship I saw close up after my parents' that was unstable and toxic. Their life together was full of turmoil, violence, and instability. This kind of relationship would become my "normal". Their marriage was on and off for years, and I had a front-row seat to their dysfunction. When she had her son, I started taking care of him on my breaks from school. In retrospect, that was crazy that my mother and sister thought it was perfectly acceptable for an eleven-year-old to watch an infant for the summer. I remember bathing him when he was tiny. If you had asked me, I would have said that I knew exactly what I was doing and was perfectly capable of taking care of this small child—but I was only a child myself.

Then there was my brother and his girlfriend. He was about five years her senior when they started dating; she was fourteen. It was another tumultuous relationship full of violence, drugs, and sex. Her family didn't like my brother for a number of reasons, ethnicity being one of them. My brother was extremely abusive and cruel to her, and to women in general. He was also a serial cheater like my father, and treated and spoke of women with hatred and disgust like they were sex objects. I remember hearing my brother beating his girlfriend, having sex, and getting high in his room at all times of day and night with no regard for the rest of the household members.

I didn't have anyone to show me what a healthy relationship looks like. So, by the time I was thirteen years old, I had my first boyfriend—a neighbor who was eighteen. He would be the first sexual experience I thought to be consensual. Although, the first time we had sex, I was so drunk that to this day I don't have any recollection of what happened. The only reason I knew was because I had blood in my underwear the next day, just like in the movies. This ridiculously inappropriate relationship would continue for about six months. It is bizarre to think that a grown man would want to have sex with a thirteen-year-old kid and have to get her drunk to do so. I didn't see anything wrong with the events except that I wished I remembered. I was so head over heels for this guy who looking back was clearly a pedophile.

I went on to high school where I would eventually meet the boy I would love for the next thirty years. This boy and I shared some of the most traumatic moments of our lives during our two-year romance. He was the only man who treated me with love, kindness, and respect despite being only seventeen years old. In the same year, he lost his brother and cousin to gun violence, while I would lose myself to an act of violence by my brother. That young man showed me what love could look like in a way I'd never seen before and I would take that with me for the rest of my life. The romance wouldn't survive our youth, my trauma, or the turmoil in my heart and mind…but I would pine for him for the rest of my adult life.

I would go on to experience excess of everything, alcohol, drugs, sex, and violence, for the rest of my youth into my adult relationships. My first physically abusive relationship happened when I was about seventeen dating a twenty-four-year-old. This man ushered me into the type of relationship I was most comfortable with. It was full of abuse on many levels, but most I wouldn't understand or even recognize for many years to come. This was simply my comfort zone because it's what I'd known my entire life. This abusive relationship with a man looked exactly what my parents', my brother's, and my sister's relationships all looked like. I'd be stuck in this new cycle of abuse for the next year or so. In fact, I moved out of my mother's house to go live with this man purely out of desperation to get away from my immediate family—mostly my brother. I returned after six months. The street life we led full of drugs, alcohol, and violence was just as bad as being at home with my family. I decided that at least at home with my crappy family, I wouldn't go to jail for living with a drug dealer. Also, I wouldn't be getting beatings, cigarette burns, or senseless terror from someone I didn't even like with no prospects for a better future.

My high school experience was a reflection of my life…it was inconsistent and meaningless with little success. I learned next to nothing during high school. I barely graduated with no intentions or motivation to attend college. In fact, my guidance counselor advised me to drop chemistry when I was failing because I didn't need college prep courses since I wasn't going to college anyway. That was her advice without ever discussing college or any other opportunities with me.

I met Johnny six months later.

---

**REFLECTIONS FROM RECOVERY**

» Trauma and coping mechanisms show up in all aspects of our lives. They show up in every interaction we have with the world from its people to the environment. The trauma affects how we think of ourselves and how we perceive people while our coping mechanisms determine how we respond. One of the initial steps in the healing journey is forgiving ourselves for what we did in survival. Another critical step is being honest about which coping mechanisms still serve us today and which ones must change. In part, there is an accountability process where we determine how we are negatively affecting our present by holding onto our past.

» Migrating to a new country causes trauma which may be obvious to some but it wasn't to me because it is so normalized. In addition to the fear and anxiety caused by the process of being misplaced, children of immigrant parents are often parentized by the responsibilities of helping parents who do not speak the language of the new country navigate the environment. Those same children often have to learn to deal with adult subjects.

» Poverty and food insecurity cause trauma. A child that grows up unsure of where their next meal will come from is in a constant state of hypervigilance and fear. Food is a basic need and not having enough food is a constant threat to living.

» Therapy is the best place to unpack childhood trauma because it is a safe place. Ideally, your therapist will guide you through the process in a way that won't be overwhelming. The reason what happened is traumatic is because our minds couldn't process it. It is critical you process it in a way that is tolerable otherwise it will just be more trauma. A therapist can validate your feelings, helping you find healthy coping mechanisms and help you feel safe enough to process.

» Many of the patterns in our romantic relationships are learned behaviors from childhood that we learn from our parents or guardians. We don't only learn from the parent that is present. We often learn as much from the parent that is absent. Our parent's absence can help create many fears of losing love that will plague all our close and particularly romantic relationships. Many people create walls, self sabotage or just avoid intimacy all together our of fear to lose love again.

» We interpret our parents' unresolved trauma as conditional love because it shows up in their vocabulary and the way they express their love. Just like we were completely dependent on our parents as children. They were completely dependent on theirs who were often in a state of survival. To further exasperate, societal norms have often played a critical part in how we parent. When looking at our societal norms we have to be critical and remember that societal norms are created to further a narrative that helps only some. For example, it was once normal to have slavery, for women to be treated as property and for adult men to child brides. Physical violence against children was often referred to as an important part of parenting.

### RECOMMENDED RESOURCES AND INFORMATION
**Books**
» *How to Do the Work* by Dr. NiDylan LePera
» *What Happened to You* by Oprah Winfrey and Dr. Bruce D. Perry

**Sites**
» Adverse Childhood Experiences (ACES) quiz: https://americanspcc.org/take-the-aces-quiz/
» Maslow's Hierarchy of Needs | Simply Psychology: https://www.simplypsychology.org/maslow.html

## Chapter 5 - What Came Before

    Family is so extraordinarily complicated. We love them because they share our lives during the most critical and influential years or because we desperately want to be a part of something. It is not uncommon for siblings to dislike each other and for people to hold many grudges against their parents. It is hard to determine the difference between love, familiarity, and the societal expectations of what a family should look like. From the perspective of my own childhood, family looked fucked up. My family experiences are full of neglect, betrayal, and abuse. The most interesting part of the story is that I didn't know the depth of the pain and trauma until just recently.

    My mother has been this constant shadow in my head that weaves in and out of all my thoughts. The sense of shame, guilt, and conditional love she instilled in me will be with me forever. She was a constant in my life, so I am sure some of my good traits come from her as well. When I think of her experiences growing up and as an adult, I want to take my hat off to her; however, when I think of her impact on my life, I want to yell at her. My grandmother, who was also a strong determined woman like my mother and me, was the product of even worse circumstances.

    My grandmother was raised by strangers after her mother died when she was four. When her father remarried, she and a couple of her siblings were adopted out. She was taken into the home of a local family and became like their maid, washing clothing until her fingers were raw in exchange for food and a place to sleep. Another woman saw how she was treated and took her to live with her family to raise and to help her. It's not likely that she ever went to school, but this woman taught my grandmother to be a seamstress, which was how she supported her family into adulthood. Unfortunately, in that home my grandmother was molested and became pregnant by the age of fifteen by the woman's eighteen-year-old son who lived in the house. She had a second child out of wedlock by the age of eighteen, which in the '40s automatically made a woman a whore. She had no parents to care for her or protect her from anything or anyone.

My grandmother was pretty amazing with me, but she was a dysfunctional parent. She managed to raise my aunt and mother as a single parent with little-to-no support, but it was rough. She had an extremely volatile relationship with the father of her children and was highly abusive. She had no role models or even the faintest idea of how to be a mother. She was verbally abusive with her kids and would make fun of their bodies. She also used physical abuse as a form of punishment. She never had anyone to teach her how to parent or be a role model for her, so she did the best she could.

I really don't know my grandmother's full story. I know only the few details she shared with me when she was helping to raise me. I wish I would have asked more questions, but I didn't think I should or could. I do know that she learned how to read and write at the age of thirty after she migrated to the US from Costa Rica in the '60s with only her daughter, my aunt. She worked her fingers to the bone and was an amazing grandmother to me. It was really sad to see how much pain my mother carried as a result of my grandmother's abuse. It serves as the perfect example of the effects of generational trauma.

My mother worked so hard to be different than my grandmother when raising. She wasn't physically abusive, and she was extraordinarily forgiving and kind. However, she still used guilt, shame, and emotional blackmail to control her children. Of all her good and bad traits, it was her inability to connect with me emotionally and her neglect that hurt the most. I don't remember much about our relationship when I was young. I do remember feeling a lot of resentment toward her early in life. I think that by the time I came around, my dad's abuse had already taken its toll on her, and she had little left to give me. She stayed at home with me and met my basic needs such as clothing me, feeding me, and coming to my aide when I got hurt, but she wasn't available emotionally. She was in too much of her own pain and working too hard to survive to worry about much else.

After my parents divorced and my mother started to hang out and party with my fifteen-year-old sister and her circle of friends, I was left to my own devices, and

I was really not equipped to figure things out for myself surrounded by adult situations at only six years old. Anxiety, lack of safety, and constant fear became part of my emotional arsenal. And so, my lifelong battle with loving and hating my mother began. I have spent the last forty years struggling with this constant pain, mostly unconsciously. It hasn't been until the last year or so, actively working through my childhood trauma and educating myself as much as possible on generational trauma, that I have been able to see her as just another flawed human being without the anger, resentment, and disappointment that I held onto for so long.

My relationship with my grandmother on the other hand was positive. She gave me a safe place to land when I was incredibly vulnerable. She gave me room to be more of myself than I had anywhere else. I felt her love unconditionally, which was more than I'd ever known. The time I spent with her really solidified my presence on this earth. She gave me a strength that has carried me through the worst times. She was tough and kind all at once. She was the strongest woman I've ever known. She was remarkable; although, she was also the woman who broke my mother and made her the woman I once hated more than life itself. Generational trauma is so complex and layered that it takes so much energy to understand; however, understanding it gives freedom like no other. Understanding is the first step in healing.

My sister is definitely my mother's daughter. She is ultra relaxed in a way that makes me uncomfortable; however, I will say she has tried to do right by her daughter—though I do wish she would have been a better role model for me. When we were young, she struggled in the same ways I did, although it manifested itself differently. She too engaged in risky behavior, had abusive relationships, and had significant self-esteem issues. She is incredibly passive and avoids conflict whenever possible. It is amazing how she avoided independence, success, and stability by maintaining complete co-dependency with my mother. I loved her at many times through our lives for the same qualities I loved in my mother. She is kind, forgiving, and non-judgmental...which I also sometimes hated. Her unconditional forgiveness came from her avoidance of conflict. Her kindness was a result of her need for approval. Her non-judgmental manner was really her inability to take a stand or position on anything to avoid conflict. Still, those qualities are admirable in anyone and were what I needed at different points in my life.

The seven-year age difference between my sister and me impacted our relationship in complicated ways. I learned early that I had to work for attention, acceptance, and love, even from my sister. I had to fit into her world in order for her to see me. Unfortunately, that meant I had to live in a world I was not ready for. The dynamic started early in our relationship going back to Costa Rica. It was evident that I had to act beyond my age and be extraordinary in order to be valued by her. I don't blame her for that, she didn't know how to love me as I was. She was a kid herself and struggled with some of the same pain I did. Also, because of the age difference, we had very different experiences with our parents. She occasionally attempted to push back to make me act my age, but I knew that acting my age came with a price and that I would lose her attention and companionship.

The dynamic continued to manifest itself throughout our lives, both she and my mother encouraged me to sexualize early. I dressed like a grown woman when I was just a kid, and I was constantly put into adult situations. The worst part was that no one prepared me to deal with these situations. I didn't have the language or maturity to handle adult men sexualizing me and taking advantage of me. We frequented bars, dance clubs, adult parties, and other situations where alcohol was easily accessible, and I was constantly surrounded by grown men. It was a lot for a kid to grapple with all while experiencing sexual harassment in every part of my life—at home, at school, and later at work. I just can't imagine how I was supposed to handle situations like this instinctually, particularly when my early cries for help were minimized and trivialized.

The dynamic between my sister and I was similar to the dynamic I eventually developed with my brother. My brother and I didn't have any sort of relationship until I moved to the US. He was ten years older than me, and, in my eyes, he became the father figure I lacked. Initially, he took a strong interest in me in a very protective and familial way. He bought me Christmas presents, took me to the movies, and just hung out with me—he allowed me to actually be a child.

I had a few distant family members who attempted to nurture the child in me; however, it became harder and harder as I started claiming that I was an adult when I was as young as twelve. In retrospect, claiming adulthood seems like a very normal thing for a child at that age, but that is the moment when adults should intervene. I don't think that, initially, anyone meant any harm, I think it was just easier to give into the situation because it required less effort. Making space for a child among all those adults would have taken a whole lot of effort from adults who themselves were struggling.

My brother was a functioning alcoholic and drug addict. He drank every day openly in the house, and he was vulgar and temperamental. Although I don't remember much about my father, I imagine that he was probably the same way. Eventually, the violence followed. My brother was very violent with his girlfriend and didn't make much of an effort to hide it. I remember hearing him beating her in his bedroom. We could all hear him, and the most my mother would do if it was really out of control was to knock and tell him to stop. We could also hear them having sex at all times of the day. Violence, sex, and drugs were staples in my house. My mother attempted to deny it was happening by ignoring it. She was so overcome by guilt and didn't know how to deal with it.

My brother and I mostly remained close despite the circumstances. We definitely gravitated towards each other. I am not sure why he gravitated toward me; I think he really did become a substitute for my dad—or at least, I unconsciously wanted him to. His role as protector was short-lived, and soon we became buddies. Like my mother and sister, it was easier to treat me as though I was older and bring me into his world instead of coming down to my level. What this meant for me was access to alcohol, sexualization, and witnessing violence. Being exposed to this type of environment by all my trusted adults gave me a false sense of what I could and should be able to handle. The reality was that I didn't know how to handle any of it, and what I considered to be failed attempts became additional points of shame and self-hatred. I also started to build resentment towards my family in a very deep part of my mind.

I have some very clear and vivid memories of my brother and our "bonding". I remember he bought me Barbies for my first Christmas in the US. He often took me as his alibi when he cheated on his girlfriend. I would lie for him, of course. He let me drink early on, even before my sister did. He took me to the movies when I was really young to watch inappropriate movies full of violence and sex. To me, it was bonding time and time outside the house; I don't know what it was to him. Perhaps he just didn't know how to relate to me or how to interact with a kid. I would imagine we all shared some type of trauma from our family and none of us knew how to really be children or feel safe.

Our relationship fluctuated throughout the years. I would find other interests with people my own age but would gravitate back to my siblings from time to time. We lived together or within a close perimeter throughout my entire youth. I guess we were a tight-knit family held together by guilt, shame, and trauma. The family never had a shortage of drama, conflict, and messiness. It was common for emergencies to pop up often even though, in our own ways, we each looked to have stability. The emergencies were often a result of the chaos, poverty, reckless lifestyles, and deep trauma. My brother was extremely disrespectful to my mother, sister, and me, so although they often tried to avoid conflict, it was always there.

On the night that changed my relationship with my brother and my life forever, he was bewildered when I saw him. He'd been drinking and doing drugs for hours, but I didn't realize that I was in danger until it happened. I truly believed that he would always see me as his sister, even if not as a child. I wonder if my sister knew he would cross the line…I wonder if he ever crossed the line with her. Under the circumstances, it doesn't seem like an impossible event.

After that night, we wouldn't speak again for almost ten years. It wasn't until my mother declared that he was welcome in her house while I was living there. It was difficult to adjust to this new situation immediately after I left Johnny. I was still recovering from all the trauma from years of extremely physical abuse to now have to coexist in harmony with my attacker in my home. It happened gradually. Initially, he would just occasionally stop by my mother's house to visit; however, over time, he became a staple. He somehow made his way back into the family unit despite his past sins. It made me feel unseen, unheard, and unloved. The pain ran deep, but I had to push it down as far as I could. I had no time for feelings, anger, or resentment. I had to survive to get my kids away from that family—but I had no idea how.

At one point, I had pushed the pain and memories so far down in my mind that it was almost as if it didn't happen. There were times when I questioned my reality and memory during those years. The one thing that I could never question was the pain I felt deep in my soul; the pain that rocked me to my core and shattered any chance I had at self-love, safety, or trust. That event was by far more painful than any pain I have felt in my life. More painful than the extreme physical abuse I faced from Johnny. More painful than the many men who betrayed and belittled me. More painful than my stepfather's psychological abuse. More painful than my father's abandonment. More painful than Kevin's narcissistic abuse. It was, by far, the one place in my heart that would never heal.

It would take years of trauma work to find the courage to say: no more. Saying no more came with many obstacles and consequences. I had to have really tough conversations with my mother and sister, and most of all, cut my brother out of my life forever. Cutting him out was not the hard part; the hard part was dealing with the guilt and shame I'd been carrying for years. I was carrying his shame and his guilt as if I'd been the one to assault him. Saying it out loud and acting on it would give me a new sense of self and freedom. It was as though the boulder that held me underwater while I drowned was suddenly lifted off. I was finally able to see myself again and maybe even love myself for the first time ever.

My father had been so absent from my life that you would think he plays no role in my story; however, it all begins with him. I have so few memories of him within the family unit. For years, I had aggrandized these memories of our outings to the beach or pool after the divorce. I held onto memories of happiness, laughter, and safety. Now I realize that the core memories are the ones of violence. It was so much less painful to romanticize our father-daughter dynamic into some loving relationship. The reality was that he was an abuser of my mother, brother, and sister. I never experienced his wrath, but only because I was too young to provoke that type of reaction.

The terrible part of coming to these realizations is that I really desired the connection and yearned for his affection. I walked away from our life in Costa Rica at eight years old with an empty space deep in my heart. I had to make up stories to survive the pain and protect myself. I have seen my father maybe seven times in the past forty years. Each visit would last seven to fourteen days max. How does a father connect with their child in that type of timeline? How do you connect with someone you don't live life with or rarely see? How do you connect with someone who doesn't know what you struggle with? How do you connect with someone when all your interactions are superficial, brief, and full of unresolved feelings?

Each time I saw my father, feelings of pain and loss flooded through me. The joy of the possibility of a real connection and love was right in front of me but never came to fruition. Instead, I got to say goodbye each time and relive the pain and trauma all over again. All the what-ifs played in my head over and over again. What if I would have had a father to protect me, to see me for who I am, to love me unconditionally, or just to let me know I am not broken and I am deserving of love? Would I have not been molested? Would I have not been abused? Would I have not been raped? Would I have been a better version of myself? The reality is that, because of the person he was, the same or worse things might have happened. But, it doesn't matter because I will never know.

All of these circumstances, relationships, and dysfunction were what set the stage for my life. A life of pain, adversity, and survival. People often say you are stronger for it, and the truth is that I would have been amazing regardless. The adversity and strength it took to overcome all this could have been used toward greater things. I would have been smart, hardworking, driven, enthusiastic, and full of radiant energy no matter what. I would have done great work anyway. The pain didn't make me more empathetic or a better person—it almost killed me. I overcame it because my light was shining bright enough to help me out of the darkness in my mind and heart.

### REFLECTIONS FROM RECOVERY
- Our parents love you, they just didn't have to tools to deal with their own trauma.
- They often tried to do it different than their own parents but didn't know how.
- They couldn't deal with their own trauma because they didn't have the tools.
- They didn't know that most of their action were unconscious.
- Therapy is the best place to unpack generation trauma although it is incredibly painful initially.
- Recognizing our parents' trauma is painful.

## Chapter 6 - Breaking the Cycle

Each child is their own world. Their minds, bodies, and souls are unique and fragile. It will take a person a lifetime of work to feel fulfilled as a parent and satisfied with their work. Children are all consuming and bring so much joy; however, what we as parents often see, besides the loves of our lives, is a reflection of our shame and guilt and the unraveling of our mistakes. Why are we so controlling and hard on our children? Usually, it's because we are afraid they will make the mistakes that we made and were never able to fix.

I have five of those individual worlds, each with their own unique personality, experiences, and needs. The love I feel for each of my children is larger than life. The amount of effort it has taken to get them to this point on my own, and often against the adult men in our lives, has been immeasurable. Kari, Bee, and Sebastian are the children I had with Johnny. I later had Kyle and Dylan with Kevin. All five are my best work as a human and a mother. It's amazing how different they can be when they were all raised by the same parent. Unfortunately, they were also all negatively affected by my toxic relationships with men. It is hard to see the good I did in raising them when the mistakes are so blinding.

I had Kari just a few months after my twenty-first birthday. She was a gift from the universe. Kari was beautiful, solemn, and loved me unconditionally. I am not sure how quickly and at what point we developed a mutual emotional co-dependency for each other. She became my reason for living, and I became her crutch. My baby was my everything. She is a product from the rawest parts of me. She had the no college education, no guidance, no focus Nancy. She grew in a pure unrefined love that was equally good and painful. Kari also represented all of my mother's mistakes with me, that I repeated with her, and the guilt and shame that resulted.

Kari was an amazing child. She was quiet, exceptionally well behaved, and always with me. She witnessed so much abuse from conception. She was also the recipient of the most love I could give to any one person. Kari was the largest child I gave birth to, and she remains the tallest female in our family. She was taller than most kids in her school, plus she was curvy—a tough mix in early childhood through high school, especially when you are one of the few minorities in town.

Kari also had to deal with my full crazy before I knew about self-awareness, conscientious parenting, or generational trauma. I poured all my love into to her while I also lived in a constant state of anxiety and fear. Kari learned early on to manage her own emotions in order to readily tend to my needs.

Bee was born when Kari was about nineteen months old. That age difference was critical to their relationship, and Kari took on a parental role almost immediately. By the time Kari was only three and Bee was one, Kari was changing her diaper and holding her hand to help her walk. It was instinctual but also necessary; somehow Kari knew I was at full capacity with Johnny. Their relationship would continue to have this dynamic into adulthood. Kari's instinct to self-abandon and give her all to help all others would become a theme through her life—always willing to give, even when it was a detriment to her happiness and well-being.

Although her school years were tough, full of bullying, being an outsider, and a lack of friendships beyond her cousin and sister, her artistic talents flourished early. I had evidence of her gift as early as kindergarten. Luckily, despite my lack of resources or good parenting skills, I knew that encouraging her was critical and so I started early on. She continued to excel within her craft into high school. She developed her creative talent through several channels. She fought and resisted Kevin's attempts to crush her—at her own expense by developing unhealthy coping mechanisms like many of us. Her outlet for her pain became food. It became her drug of choice to help her find the satisfaction and control she lacked in most aspects of her life.

As early adulthood hit, Kari's self-awareness and search for healing became more important than ever. Her struggle with food and her art were just small parts of who she was. Soon, she began to develop her sense of self and a strong voice that drowned out all the bullshit from the world. Kari became her own person full of opinions, talents, achievements, imperfections, and, most of all, immense love. Seeing her grow has been one of the biggest pleasures of my life.

Bryanna, or Bee as we often call her, is so incredibly different and unique that it makes it hard to believe that I raised both sisters. Bee was born right before my twenty-third birthday. Her pregnancy was incredibly difficult because the reality of having another child with Johnny was overwhelming, and it sent me into full denial. I barely acknowledged my pregnancy until I was forced to confront it. It was difficult to connect with a baby I felt would give him more leverage over me. The first six months of her life were full of postpartum depression, colic, and emotional turmoil. I would sit with Bee in my arms and Kari next to me and just weep in complete sorrow. It was such a sad time for me. I felt defeated as a person and a mom. How could I have betrayed these two little girls by bringing them into a world with a man like Johnny in their lives? At the time, I had accepted that my life would be riddled with violence and pain forever. That realization included a life of pain and violence for my babies. What kind of mother would do that?

Bee learned to lean on Kari early on, reinforcing their relationship of child and protector. As a little girl, Bee was incredibly shy and quiet with the occasional angry outburst. She was mostly very obedient but occasionally pushed back hard with full enthusiasm regardless of the consequences. She started to push boundaries early. By the age of six, she'd already threatened to run away. I responded by packing her bags and asking her where I should drop her off since I was the only person she had in the world—my mother of the year moment. Interactions of this nature would go on to create fears within her about my safety and well-being. I am sure that witnessing episodes of violence from Johnny didn't help.

As Bee entered grammar school and later middle school, she worked harder and harder to become independent from Kari. She developed a lot of friendships, some remaining into adulthood. Bee had a small frame, was short and athletic, giving her a very different experience from Kari. She was popular and sort of a mean girl fueled by all the insecurities that resulted from the violence Kevin brought into our lives during her critical years. Middle school was tough for us. Bee wanted more independence, and I and really worked hard to ensure she wasn't hidden in our shadows. She wanted to find herself, which sometimes showed up as anger and frustration, and often resulted in her cutting off from the family. By high school, Bee was fully independent from Kari, and their relationship became rocky.

Bee would struggle the next few years in a strong attempt to find her own voice, passion, and purpose. Eventually, she found a job at a daycare and started spending time with us again, reconnecting with her siblings, and it seemed to help her reconnect with herself. She seemed happier, or at least more grounded, as she started to find her way back to herself. While working and after encountering a few health issues, she conceived her first baby girl. It appears that, much like me, motherhood gave Bee purpose and direction. Slowly, I could see that starting her own family and understanding her place within it helped her make sense of the world.

Soon, Bee developed into a strong partner to her boyfriend and an amazing mom to her baby girl. She seemed clearer than ever; although, anxiety would haunt her with postpartum and in her everyday living. The anxiety was starting to manifest in a new way, and now she was learning to recognize it for what it was. In the past, she had addressed it much like I addressed mine when I was young: through partying, drinking, and people. She was now learning to feel what was happening within her body, but it would likely take time for her to understand why—which was obvious to me with our history of domestic violence and abuse.

Sebastian was my third child with Johnny. He doesn't know it, but he is the one who gave me the final push to leave. A therapist told me while I was pregnant with Sebastian that Johnny would do to him all the grotesque things Johnny's father had done to him. It scared me into reality, and I decided that I would leave him at any cost—and so the plotting began. By the time Sebastian was two weeks old, I was waiting for the opportunity to spring into action, and when it did, I was ready. I had finally decided that it was my kids or him, and my kids would win every time.

Sebastian had an extremely different experience from the girls. While I was able to get him away from Johnny's extreme violence, I also wasn't emotionally available to him. I was in full survival mode, which meant I had no energy or emotional capacity for a baby. All his physical needs were taken care of, and others gave him love; however, I wasn't fully present for him. I loved him dearly with the love I had available. I was desperate to give him and his sisters a different experience than the one I had. When he was born, I was twenty-five and on welfare with no college education or direction.

Sebastian was very much a typical little boy: rambunctious, curious, and mischievous. The girls were not exactly receptive to a little boy who was several years younger and so different from them. His relationship with them was likely typical but became tumultuous due to all the abuse that followed when Kevin joined the family. Sebastian was diagnosed with ADHD at six, which gave him a very negative educational experience. He was riddled with insecurities, trauma, and challenges that arose from lack of understanding and support. I didn't give him enough support or reassurance, while the school failed him completely. He became obsessed with his appearance as a way of coping with those insecurities, and Kevin exploited them to maintain. The truth is that Kevin was incredibly jealous of mine and Sebastian's relationship as it grew, and also of Sebastian's potential. He hated Sebastian because he was all he wanted and could never be.

Sebastian struggled all through middle school and high school with mediocre grades and Kevin's constant abuse. He never felt safe—at home, he walked on eggshells all the time because triggering Kevin was like setting off a train, and at school, he was always afraid of his peers finding out he had ADHD because he didn't understand what he was dealing with. The resources the school gave him didn't meet his needs and the bullying culture put him in a constant state of anxiety. All these things put together were a perfect recipe for a terrible experience.

By his senior year of high school, he was full of pent-up anger and distrust. My few attempts to connect were too little too late and the damage was far too much. I was constantly afraid Kevin would use any excuse to make a real attempt to hurt him. During one of Sebastian's temper tantrums that was full of yelling and cursing at me, I responded by kicking him out of the house. At the time, I believed I had saved him from Kevin, believing he would be back shortly. It didn't go the way I expected. Instead, he moved in with my mother where he would stay for at least three years.

During those years, he tried desperately to find his way, working many different menial jobs. He refused to go into the military, even though I tried profusely to convince him to go. He worked really hard to find who he was deep inside and to understand his challenges. He became fixated with ADHD and understanding his diagnosis. Finding himself was his purpose; however, he didn't know it yet. The many years of abuse had taken their toll on him in every way. His self-hatred, shame, and guilt were a constant in his body not allowing him to grow or connect with others despite his constant attempts to do so.

During this time, he tried to bond with me, but neither of us were ready for true connection. The love between us was palpable, but the connection was inconsistent at best. He would text me occasionally professing his love and admiration; however, it always felt forced and unauthentic. He struggled with outbursts of anger and aggression at my mother's house fueled by their messy home life. He lived in her basement where he shared space with my nephew who was twenty years older than him and in a worse state. It was a difficult time for him on top of an already difficult life. He spent those three years figuring out his direction and how to cope with his challenges.

By the time he was twenty-one, he started coming into his own. He figured out he wanted to work in healthcare and picked an educational path. He became more and more informed about ADHD, giving him the tools to go to college with a small sense of confidence. In late 2019, when Kevin was taken away by the police after his last attempt to physically hurt me, Sebastian finally moved back home. Moving back home suddenly allowed him the space to feel his emotions, identify his feelings, and recognize the anxiety his body had been riddled with for years. The challenges that come with healing were many, but he was determine to get there.

Kyle was eleven years later. He was born when I was thirty-six just after a miscarriage that rocked my world. His was my only planned pregnancy, and it was by far the scariest in terms of the baby's well-being. The miscarriage was so traumatic that having another baby triggered every fear in me. That pregnancy was all the things a pregnancy should not be. Kevin was incredibly emotionally and physically abusive at a different level. Johnny was abusive in an overt way, but Kevin's abuse was subtle and far more damaging because most of it was focused on my mind. He gaslighted me regularly and made me question my worth at every turn, particularly after the miscarriage, which I am convinced he caused. On top of all that, I was the bread winner and experienced health complications.

When Kyle was born, I was delighted and filled with relief. My baby was healthy despite all the ruthless shit his father had done to me during the pregnancy. Kyle was an incredibly good baby in a different way than I recognized. He was unusually quiet and was soothed by sound much more than by touch. His awareness was different from other young children; he picked up on energy in a different way. Luckily for him, my mother took over as his nanny after six months, relieving Kevin and allowing him to do nothing. I had gone back to work after only two months, which made my mother's care critical.

By the time Kyle was two years old, I started to see that he had unique needs. He was deathly afraid of crowds, strangers, and new activities, and he already showed a particular fixation with patterns. He spent countless hours on all forms of electronics—television, iPad, toys, phones. He also spent endless hours rewatching the same episodes of cartoons and music videos or rereading the same books. He became obsessed with organizing items in patterns such as cards. Unfortunately, Kevin would not even entertain the idea that Kyle might have a developmental challenge or other abilities. In fact, he loved that Kyle was a homebody because it allowed him to hide behind it while making no effort to be a dad.

I put what I saw in my back pocket and encouraged Kyle to "come out of his shell". I took him to parks and other places he didn't like and pushed him into physical activity. I enrolled him in basketball, swimming, and karate. Eventually, I sent him to daycare to have more interaction with other kids and more stimulation as my mother was no longer helping him. She didn't know how and, much like Kevin, enjoyed his calm and lack of physical activity due to her age. Kyle didn't enjoy daycare; however, it was a window into his life from a different lens. The daycare teacher reaffirmed Kyle's challenges and gave me the confidence to pursue a diagnosis despite Kevin's resistance.

The social challenges weren't the only unique aspect of Kyle's development. By age three, he taught himself how to read, learned how to count to ten in French, and could count up to one thousand on his own. His intellectual development was extremely advanced for his age, and although I was proud, I knew I needed to understand his development to ensure his needs were met. Kevin was a combination of supportive and dismissive. He never lifted a finger to help, but always showed up playing the part of the concerned parent. It was incredibly frustrating and put so much more pressure on me. Meanwhile, Kyle was struggling with typical experiences like going to the mall, carnivals, dining out, and learning to swing.

By the time he was four, I'd worked with his pediatrician to get him a diagnosis—autism—and so his new journey began. Kyle continues to be an exceptional child. He accepts help, although it is difficult for him to admit he needs it. He has developed in the areas that were challenging for him beautifully. He has learned acceptable social skills while still maintaining his uniqueness. He is amazingly clever and has a sense of humor that is witty and fast. He has an outstanding vocabulary and general knowledge in many subjects. He is also incredibly empathetic and sensitive to conflict. His empathy is almost detrimental and makes him vulnerable to predators like Kevin.

Kyle's school experience was mostly positive although there were the occasional struggles like any other kid. It was a welcome surprise that he was able to adjust so well. He learned to make the best of the experience while receiving great services. It helped that his sisters acquired a great deal of knowledge regarding child development. Both girls became an intricate part of his development and a strong support system for me. The help was highly welcome since Kevin was the opposite of helpful. He was threatened when I focused too much on the kids, even his own biological child. He was bothered by my constant efforts to push Kyle out of his comfort zone to help his development. The girls were my only allies in the effort to help Kyle find his potential.

In retrospect, he was exposed to Kevin's abuse since he was in the womb. Kevin was most physically abusive during the first three years of our relationship. The first time he was physically abusive was while I was pregnant with the baby I miscarried. The abuse intensified during Kyle's pregnancy and immediately after. He continued to be abusive for the following five years; however, the frequency of the abuse decreased over time. It became less necessary for him to be physically abusive because I became more compliant. By that point, Kyle had already been exposed to years of violence during his most vulnerable and fragile years.

All the hostile and aggressive behavior leading up to the announcement of the divorce had already put Kyle in a heightened state of vigilance. Kevin preys on Kyle's immense empathy through manipulation, withholding of affection, and intimidation. Although I know Kyle can see the real intentions behind many of Kevin's actions, I also know that feelings don't always align with logic. I can often see the struggle in his eyes. It is as though his intuition tells him that his dad is a bad guy, but his heart wants his love so he can't reconcile it. I understand because I experienced similar pain with my own father. All I can hope for is that he will see who he is dealing with at some point and that therapy will help him understand that it has nothing to do with him.

My youngest child is Dylan, and he is so much like me. He is incredibly aware of his surroundings, people, and intentions. He is particularly sensitive to other people's energy. He showed signs of a strong intuition when he was very young. He also has an ability to articulate his feelings in a way that is very advanced for his age., I was very close to him when he was little for a number of reasons. I knew he was the last child I would give birth to, and I was able to be more present since I was leaving my survivor state.

Although for many years I convinced myself that I had not exposed Dylan to violence or anxiety, I realize now that I did. Kevin was particularly cruel when I was pregnant or injured. It seemed that the weaker he perceived me, the more powerful he felt, which resulted in greater cruelty. Also, Kevin was still physically abusive during the first three years of Dylan's life. In fact, the violence had escalated because the more we changed as a family, the more he threatened he felt. I was of the mindset that kids didn't understand what was happening when they were young, not fully grasping that it is just as damaging as when they are older.

Dylan was a very anxious child—and, in retrospect, I can see why. Dylan cried a great deal when I left in the mornings. Kevin often FaceTimed me while I drove to work so Dylan could cry to me. Dylan's temperament was also very cyclical early on. I was not attuned enough to understand back then, but now I can see that he just needed connection. Both Kevin and my mother where emotionally unavailable to him, and I wasn't much better, but I was more present.

When I got home from work, he was typically desperate for me, which was exhausting, but he really just needed to be seen. Kevin's way of making him happy was with junk food, which just made Dylan's moods even worse. It took me time to figure out that I needed to detox him. The detox was very effective allowing him to be a much happier child. Luckily for Dylan, he spent a lot of time with me and the girls. The weekends were often spent at the beach or the park with just the girls and me. Those were the moments when he found his inner strength.

Dylan was and continues to be super shy, much like Bee and Kari. It always seems incredibly surprising to me that my kids have been shy since I was so outgoing as a child. I am not sure if that is a result of me being such an extrovert or their interactions with abusive father figures. One thing about Dylan is that he loves people and needs friends. He needs connections at a deeper level than my other kids did.

The divorce was particularly difficult on Dylan, as he was only seven, and it showed. Kevin's manipulation and his emotional abuse had taken their toll. Kevin made sure he broke him by intimidating him and giving small bouts of attention to encourage him to work for more. It was so hard to see Dylan hurt so much in the beginning. He was so angry with me because he felt abandoned. It was clear his pain was overwhelming, and I was the easiest target. I knew he felt safest here so he could act out and show his emotions with me and Bee at the time.

The first time he came home for dinner after spending days with Kevin, Dylan wouldn't let me touch him. He wouldn't let me even caress his hair. It was so sad and painful to see him in so much pain. He cried desperately and isolated himself from all of us. He looked to Kyle for comfort, but Kyle didn't have the tools or awareness to understand what his brother was going through. Dylan's devastation was palpable. My heart ached, and I would feel his pain in every part of my body. It was devastating for all of us. Poor Dylan had to develop his own coping mechanisms. One was putting space between him and me. He didn't let me give him affection for a long time, and he wouldn't tell me he loved me. Instead, he tried to fill the void with material things like toys. His other outlet was his friends, though his father often stood in the way of him maintaining strong friendships.

Today, Dylan has come a long way. He is much more at peace and has found new outlets. The goal is to keep him as busy as possible when he is with Kevin and to love him as much as possible when he is here. It is difficult because when he is here, he uses the same coping mechanisms he uses at Kevin's house, where he is allowed to have excessive amounts of time on electronics. I focus on encouraging him to spend more time with his friends and be active and away from screens. We have also seen improvement in our relationship. He tells me he loves me again, and he also lets me give him affection and occasionally hugs me, which feels amazing.

Overall, the kids are coming along well, and I feel less and less guilty for my shortcomings as a mom each day. I am learning that although I didn't always get it right, I tried incredibly hard every day. Many of my mistakes were a result of my past baggage and not a reflection of my devotion or love. I am sure that the kids will still have grievances, but I think that is a very normal part of parent-child relationships. They will learn throughout life that although we expect our parents to be perfect and have all the answers, we don't. Parents are just people carrying their own pain, and some of us figure it out early enough to help our kids while others never figure it out. And truthfully, resources, preparation, books, or money are not what ultimately make a difference. It is healing from the past that makes us better parents. We are so much more emotionally available to our kids once we've healed, and that is what they need. Not to say that having time, money, and resources isn't important, but without emotional availability, it means nothing.

To me, the most important part of healing was self-forgiveness, acceptance, and self-love. I had to forgive myself first, which allowed me to put my ego away and stop trying to prove that it wasn't my fault. The guilt and shame made me so defensive that I couldn't see that my kids' pain was about them, not me. Whenever they were in pain, I unconsciously worked harder to show them I wasn't wrong or bad instead of allowing them to feel their emotions. It also didn't allow me to teach them healthy coping mechanisms because I didn't have any to show them. Once I forgave myself, I was able to give them room for their own pain, which allowed them to feel seen.

The acceptance followed once I forgave myself. I was able to accept myself as I am without focusing on what I'm not. Once I accepted my whole self, I was able to accept my kids as individuals instead of extensions of me. I was able to let go of who I wanted them to be and of imposing that pressure on them. Accepting me meant I could accept them, and therefore, they could accept themselves—or at least know let them know that I did. When we are kids, we need our parents' acceptance to know we are lovable. When our parents can't do that for themselves, they send us the message that we are not acceptable.

Lastly, loving myself allowed me to love them freely and unconditionally. How could I have loved them fully when I didn't love me? I made them. I gave them life in my body but hated my body. How could I love who they were and will become when I hate the mom who raised them? Loving me also allowed my gift—love—to flourish and flow into all my relationships, especially the most important ones. Loving my kids for who they are allowed me to see them, and it took all the pressure out of our relationships. It all became easier: loving them, communicating with them, and allowing them the room they need to grow beyond me.

Unfortunately, I couldn't heal and experience the changes I needed until I felt safe. I didn't feel safe until I was financially stable and away from my abusers. The fear of poverty and all the insecurities and fears that brought me in my youth plus interacting with my abusers was so hard I could never heal. I was consistently in survival mode and full of shame for not having the strength to stand up to them. It took a lot of work to understand how much I was suppressing, and how it was literally destroying me emotionally and physically. I am so grateful for the opportunity to love my five babies now, while they are still young enough for it to make a positive difference.

**REFLECTIONS FROM RECOVERY**
- » Unconscious parenting and conscious parenting look very different.
- » Shame and guilt rule most of our parenting decisions.
- » Learned behaviors result in guilt and shame and then we over compensate.
- » Apologizing to kids when we make mistakes is critical.
- » If we can't control our behaviors and we are teaching our kids how to control their behaviors what are they suppose to learn.
- » Everyone needs therapy, especially when they think they don't.
- » Therapy helps kids learn to process their emotions.

## Chapter 7 - From Surviving to Thriving

The workplace has always been the place where I shine. I overperformed in school when I was a young child and then again as an adult—and I consider school an extension of the workplace. I attended kindergarten through third grade in Costa Rica where I outperformed most kids and was incredibly independent. However, things changed drastically when I came to the US. Between the culture shock and unstable home life, my interest in school fluctuated. My effort was predicated on the interest of others more so than my own desire. Since my mother wasn't particularly engaged in my schooling, I depended on the interest of teachers or other adults outside of my family. My mother told me I was intelligent, and she expected that I would just do well. Unfortunately, because other attributes, such as my appearance, received so much more acknowledgment, they seemed much more important. I regained my interest in education as an adult—then, I shined.

I started working when I was around eleven years old babysitting my mother's coworker's two-year-old daughter. I took care of that little girl daily during the summer while her mother worked. I also started babysitting my nephew when he was still an infant. By the time I was thirteen, I had jobs outside the home.

My first job was in downtown Paterson at a teen clothing store. I lied about my age, saying I was sixteen, and used my sister's social security number, though I'm not sure why. I worked at that store for about nine months until I had a sexual encounter with the owner. I thought it was a sexual encounter at the time, but now I know it was sexual harassment and rape since I was thirteen. Even though I had lied about my age, a man in his thirties sleeping with a sixteen-year-old employee under his supervision isn't any better. After the encounter, he stopped speaking to me. I, of course, didn't have anyone to speak to about what happened, what led up to it, or how to handle something that complicated. I was so ashamed over it and the way he acted toward me afterward. These are the types of situations that can traumatize a girl or woman into a hyper-vigilant state that will ruin any aspirations for success.

I left that job when I started at Paterson Catholic High School as a freshman and replaced it with a job at a women's clothing store. I loved working there and being surrounded by professional and career-oriented women all day. All the employees were women including the managers, and they were badasses. Also, many of the women were women of color, giving me some great role models.

On Saturdays, I worked part-time at the salon where my mother worked. I did everything from washing hair to painting nails. I wasn't trained to do many of the things I did; however, I was often confident I could learn how to do anything. I learned a lot about business, specifically the kind of businesswoman I'd like to be. I remember my mother asking me if I would follow in her footsteps and become a cosmetologist. My response was always, "No, I will work in an office." I didn't know what I was going to do, I just knew early on that I would do something different.

Work is also where my mother shined. She worked more than anyone I have ever known, and her work ethic was like no other. At one point, she was working seven days a week between three different jobs. In part, it hurt me tremendously because she wasn't around for me when I really needed her emotionally. On the other hand, that's how she fed me and kept a roof over my head. She initially worked in a factory during the day, cleaned office buildings at night, and worked in a salon on the weekends for years. By the time I was in high school, she had gone to cosmetology school, gotten her license, and was working full-time at the salon in downtown Paterson where I worked with her.

Eventually, I lost my job in the women's clothing store due to transportation issues and taking too much time off when two of my close friends were killed. When it was time to find another job, one of the places I went to apply was AutoZone. It was a local store that seemed safe to just walk in and apply. The manager instructed me to fill out the application in his office while he stayed in the store. When I was done, I waited as instructed. Upon his return, he studied my application briefly and asked a few questions. He then proposed I give him oral sex in exchange for the job. I laughed it off as if he was kidding, although I knew he wasn't, politely declined, and practically ran out. I didn't tell anyone about this for some time, but it always stuck with me. I once again thought it was my fault and, therefore, felt shame over being in this situation again.

I managed to land a job at a home improvement store named Channel. I told the manager I was in college and could only work evenings and weekends. I was fifteen at this point, but I had a fake ID that said I was eighteen. I used my own identity but forged the age on the ID to avoid working papers or working hour restrictions. This job was my first window into the leader I would later become. I relished the opportunity for more responsibility and the ability to influence others. By the time I turned sixteen, I was managing five to ten nighttime cashiers and closed the store. I also ran customer service and worked audits. I loved any opportunity to be in charge, solve problems, and motivate others.

About a year into my time at Channel, the general manager came to my register on a super busy Sunday afternoon and rang up a customer. It was completely out of the norm, but he was my boss, so I let him do what he wanted. He was an older white man who rarely spoke to me, so it was pretty intimidating. Interestingly enough, my register came up $100 short when I cashed out at the end of the day. The head of security interrogated me for at least an hour. He asked me over and over what happened and why I let the manager go into the register. I was pretty scared. I was sure that no one would ever believe that I didn't take the money, but it turned out the GM had been stealing money and products for some time, and they had him on camera taking money out of my register. He was fired but not prosecuted in any way.

When I was a senior in high school, I joined a work-study program. I needed a job that would report my performance to my teacher for a grade. I was too embarrassed to tell my manager that I had lied about my age, so I decided to quit and find another job. I found a job at Sears wrapping gifts for the holidays. The day I went into the hardware store to give my two weeks' notice, my manager refused to accept my resignation and insisted I explain why I was quitting. When I admitted the truth, he laughed. He said he didn't care how old I was or if I lied, he didn't want me to quit and would sign anything for school. I stayed another year.

At Channel, I didn't experience the same level of sexual harassment that I did at my first retail job; however, I was placed in plenty of sexually exploitative situations I wasn't equipped to handle. I worked with adults who were two or three times my age who thought I was eighteen years old. I honestly don't know how they didn't know I was three years younger than I claimed—I can't imagine I was that mature. Regardless, I worked with adults that flirted with subjects I didn't know how to handle in any setting much less in the workplace.

I also partied a great deal. One of my favorite things to do when I went clubbing was dance. I participated in dance battles at NYC clubs—those were my glory days. It was by far the most fun I had as a young person. I even glued an earring to my nose because I didn't want to pierce it knowing I would work in a professional environment someday where it wouldn't be acceptable. I went clubbing up to four days a week, sometimes from Thursday through Sunday, often showing up to work with a terrible hangover. The partying rarely affected my performance, and I took great pride in my ability to work well under any circumstances. In retrospect, I am sure it did affect my overall performance, but at the time I felt like I could do anything. During my years at Channel, I had so much fun, but also lived a crazy, unpredictable life.

I quit this job to go to Florida on summer break with my abusive, drug dealing, adult boyfriend—one of many ridiculous situations. I had barely graduated high school, and then spent the next six to nine months partying until I couldn't make it through one more night. I realized that I desperately needed direction and an opportunity to exercise my ambition and drive.

I started my lifelong love for banking and leadership at the age of eighteen. The bank required a urine test, which I didn't pass the first time because of all the weed I'd been smoking with the drug dealer boyfriend. I had to get urine from a friend to pass it. Once I overcame that small obstacle, I got an entry-level teller job at a commercial bank. Within six months, I was a head teller, and in three more months, I was traveling for the bank training tellers at purchased branches. I eventually became the person who went to the new branches to determine which employees the bank would keep and which would be terminated. I enjoyed the responsibility and trust placed upon me.

I truly enjoyed the work, but my home and personal lives were a mess. I ended up quitting to work with my sister in a coffee shop that was a front for illegal gambling. This was one of the dumber things I did in my youth. I wasted a year drinking and partying again, had sex with a man who made me feel like a prostitute, and met Johnny. At this point, I desperately wanted to be saved and would have clung to anyone.

The shop was a completely toxic environment full of alcohol, caffeine, cigarettes, and all-nighters. There was some drug activity, but luckily, that was minimal. After a year, I left because Johnny demanded it. The next five years were riddled with abuse and exploitation making any dreams of a career non-existent. In fact, when I was pregnant with my first baby, Karinna, I became a recipient of Medicaid, WIC, and eventually food stamps. I felt very shameful for entering the welfare system, although it seemed very common. Johnny pressured me to do it, and with all the craziness in our lives at the time, keeping a job was virtually impossible.

I briefly attempted going to community college and working as a bank teller during those years, but Johnny made sure he destroyed every attempt at normalcy and outside interaction I made. Still, the moment he went to prison, I started planning my return to the workforce and future career options. The only career I'd ever dreamt about as a kid was being an entertainer—clearly, that wasn't happening now. When Sebastian was about six months old, I started working as a waitress, which was not ideal for me. I was not good at it, but I did it for a few months while I figured out my next move. A welfare requirement at the time was a class that went on for a few weeks that taught basic life skills and career planning. I did some research and came across the paralegal profession as a possibility. I found Berkeley College and was able to join the 4Cs county assistance program to pay for daycare for my three kids. Within months of Johnny going to prison, I was enrolled in school full time, and my enthusiasm was hard to contain. Berkeley College was scary for me, as I had barely finished high school and didn't have anyone who'd experienced college to advise me. I was on my own, yet again.

It was one of the most amazing experiences of my life. I found new enjoyment in learning, succeeding, and leadership. Leadership is my gift; it is one of the most natural talents I have. It felt as natural as breathing and sleeping. College woke up a part of me I didn't know existed. I developed a confidence in my abilities that I'd lost during my schooling experiences in both public and private school where I barely made it. Suddenly, I felt smart, as though there was nothing I couldn't learn and conquer. It felt so good to achieve again, to feel competent and accomplished. The first semester didn't go quite as planned. In fact, I was on my way to getting a C in an English class when my professor pulled me aside and reminded me of the consequences. My major had GPA requirements, and I had kids at home to take care of. This was my second chance, and there was no room for failure. It didn't take long for me to get my act together and prioritize my kids and future over all the distractions that come with being a single college student at twenty-five years old.

I managed to stay on track, but it was really challenging. The kids were so little and needed my time and attention. My family wanted to be there for me; however, they didn't know how and were unsupportive at times, though unintentionally. It was a constant battle. I was reprioritizing every day; learning to be a student after I'd spent all my school years messing around. I was not college ready and scared to death. Still, I was so optimistic and full of faith that a brighter future lay ahead. Plus, after five years of feeling like I was in prison, any path to independence and freedom seemed like the only alternative. Life was full of possibilities, and I was determined to change my kids' futures and mine. I knew that if anyone could change our situation, it had to be me.

By the second semester, I got the hang of it. I made a few friends and learned to move within society again. I spent so many years being conditioned to be careful of every interaction; I was so afraid of triggering Johnny. Even though I knew he was in prison, I constantly felt as though he was watching me. Now, I was finally in the position to learn how to socialize fearlessly and authentically. I loved life. I appreciated this second chance and was determined to succeed. At the time, I measured my success by being able to get off public assistance and providing the basic necessities for my babies.

I joined the paralegal club, student government association, and engaged in a number of other extracurricular activities. I worked a number of different jobs to make ends meet, most of which I sucked at. I was a terrible waitress and hated it. I really wanted more, but I kept reminding myself that it took baby steps.

The next eighteen months were full of late-night homework sessions, Friday nights at the McDonald's play place, and raising three beautiful kids. My niece, who was only a month younger than Karinna, also practically lived with me. Life was full, and I was young and ready for it. I remember doing laundry in the middle of the night while the kids slept. I'd get up every couple of hours to change loads. I was exhausted constantly; however, this new lease on life fueled my soul. I was determined to make it happen for my kids and me. I was determined to support my family on just my paycheck. I just wanted the basics in life. I never even dreamed of wealth or financial independence.

When I look back at those times and my accomplishments, I am in awe. Between the three very young babies, school, family chaos, and work, not losing my sanity seems like such an accomplishment. I also realize I was often not present as a parent and lived in pure survival mode for many years. During those years, I encountered many supportive individuals who helped keep me focused and encouraged.

At one point, I was asked to speak as a domestic violence survivor at a vigil with the victims of violent crimes advocacy office. I spoke in front of about three hundred people at a school auditorium. At the end of my speech, a woman came up to me, introduced herself, and offered me a job working with domestic violence victims as an advocate in court and as an educator. I leaped at the opportunity to make a difference in someone's life. It resonated with me to pay it forward, and I knew it would give my terrible experience a higher meaning. It was a great experience that would prepare me for the next few chapters of my life.

My degree required that I complete an internship, and I asked my criminal law professor to let me work with him at the Passaic County Assistant Prosecutor's office. I loved and hated it all at once. It was my first adult work experience with people I expected to be professionals, but who showed me what workplace discrimination can look like. One detective told me he lived in the same town we'd moved to a few years prior, a suburb right outside of Paterson. In that conversation, he told me that the town was changing. He went on to explain in a very disgusted tone that he was selling his house because some loud family full of kids moved into the block. We soon learned that we were neighbors and it was my family he couldn't stand to live close to. He apologized profusely, but the damage was already done. That would be one of several experiences where I felt my womanhood or ethnicity were unwelcome in a professional setting.

My next significant career stepping stone would be a finance company where I would land a job through Berkeley College's placement program. I had only one interview for an entry-level documentation position and was hired. I recall how intimidating this new environment was. I'd never worked in a professional environment made up of mostly caucasian people. I was well qualified for the work but unprepared for the people. The company grew to about 150 employees at its largest point with only a few of those employees being people of color. I often missed the signals of discrimination. One co-worker and fellow Berkeley classmate would be the person to teach me an awareness of others and the coded language. Some of the acts were incredibly overt and not requiring any interpretation—like the senior vice president who stared at my breasts any time he spoke to me as if I didn't have a face. These lessons continued throughout my time at this company.

It was particularly difficult to flourish and find opportunities when the expectations were unclear and seemed to be a moving target. For example, when I was frustrated about my manager's inability to communicate effectively, my co-worker Shawn pointed out how my manager communicated differently with certain employees. When I began to pay attention, I realized it wasn't just with me but also with the other women of color who worked in the department. Other lessons I learned were the distinct differences between wealthy people and people with low resources. This would stay with me for the rest my career. It was particularly disorienting when a person with resources or wealth discussed personal challenges that I couldn't possibly identify with. Situations like cleaning people not cleaning correctly, losing a live-in nanny, or some other wealthy person problem—or what I perceived at the time as a white person problem—that I hadn't even realized existed. I worked really hard at hiding who I was and the parts of me that were not accepted in that environment. I developed a new personality to fit within this corporate environment and saved the real me for the select few who really knew and accepted me. I created a corporate identity that was not authentic and denied many important parts of me. I genuinely didn't enjoy this change and often felt phony; however, I knew the change was necessary to gain opportunities for advancement or even to continue my employment.

I learned so many other lessons along the way. For example, I discovered that some men in this corporate environment will easily take advantage of a young desperate woman. Also, how a desperate young woman with a lot of trauma can easily confuse male inappropriate attention for connection instead of sexual harassment. It is ridiculous to realize that now, but it took me many years to learn the difference. I think a lot of it stems back to learning as a young girl that men are privileged and are not expected to have self-control. Also, we learn to laugh at the things that make us feel uncomfortable like sexual "jokes". It goes back to walking by the strip club outside my house where men stood out front and cat-called me when I was nine. If I ignored them, I was a bitch; if I engaged, I was scared because it would encourage them; and if I said something defensive, I was again a bitch. The safest bet was to avoid them or to walk fast and be afraid…don't make eye contact, don't dress too nice, don't smile, and on and on. This behavior became how I handled these types of uncomfortable situations. The other part of it was not knowing that it was wrong or inappropriate. The lack of language and mentorship made it even more difficult. I was swimming among big fish that made me feel insignificant as a woman, minority, poor person, person on public assistance, and a person lacking legacy or generational history.

Despite the many hardships, it wasn't all bad. Those lessons and my hard work started to pave the foundation for future successes and my outlook on my career. It took a lot of drive and really developing confidence in my own abilities because I definitely didn't get that from anyone in a leadership position. I had to work extra hard to stay focused and refuse to buy into the idea that I didn't deserve a seat at the table. In retrospect, this was an area where I always felt I would excel.

I enjoyed taking risks by accepting responsibility and, most of all, enjoyed problem-solving, the two strengths that would carry my career to success I would have never predicted. I took every opportunity that presented itself to learn something new and to prove myself an asset. No job was above or beneath me. I redid the file room while also writing job descriptions and working on other responsibilities I wasn't trained for. It didn't matter what it was; if it seemed challenging, I volunteered. In some cases, I did the jobs no one else would do, adding on little by little to my already overwhelming workload. It was challenging.

The next five years were critical in building my foundation in operations and critical thinking. I also went back to school for my undergrad in business management. It was one of the best decisions I ever made. Of course, it was super hard to go to school full-time, work full-time, and be a single mom of three. It was lonely and exhausting. I had a few romantic interests during that time, but for the most part, I was pretty lonely. School was wonderful for me. I loved to learn, which made my experience great while also adding to the foundation I was building. But I always felt like I was barely hanging on. There were always so many things happening. There was always a test, assignment, or event that seemed to be what would drown me. When I look back now, I am always in awe at how much I was able to overcome. I also remember the many sacrifices made. I missed so many family functions or fun outings. My youth seemed to be slipping through my fingers. I was always on edge with the kids, although, I worked extra hard to be a good mom. We had no vacations, no money, and no fancy clothes, but we still did so much. I was so determined to give them everythng I didn't have.

Berkeley College became a source of safety, pride, and excellence. By the time I returned for my undergrad, excellence was all I would accept. I became obsessed with my grades and achievements. I'd finally realized that my experiences in school during my youth were more circumstantial than about my abilities. It was nice to finally feel smart and be respected for it. It felt so good that my appearance wasn't my winning ticket anymore. I was smart and capable, which was empowering and validating. The high I achieved from winning in that environment was better than any drug in the world. I was addicted. To top it all off, I was able to use work to excel at school and vice versa.

When another bank came in and bought the bank I worked for, I got my first taste of corporate turmoil and uncertainty. There was non-stop gossiping and predictions by my peers. It was pretty scary, especially since our leaders weren't doing a good job at communicating and treated the staff like our situation wasn't as dire as theirs. As if their job loss was more important or detrimental than it was for the rest of us. You could feel the tension, and I personally made the best of it by strengthening my relationship with the big dog. I worked hard to create a channel of communication with the new CEO, which gave me a view of how big decisions are made. It made me even more confident in assuming authority and speaking on behalf of the staff.

When my time at the bank ended in May of 2005, I took a few weeks off, then started my job hunt. By July, I landed a job at a small local bank in a similar position. However, when I was hired, I was promised an opportunity to manage the team and improve the operations of the department. Once I started, I realized it was all lip service. The operation was small, with no diversity, all senior employees, and no room for development. I didn't fit in for multiple reasons, and the staff made sure I knew that. It was not a friendly place; I felt like the odd person out. As I started thinking about where I wanted to go from here, I placed my sights on law school and the LSAT, something that had been floating in the back of my mind. I started taking an LSAT class on the weekends and studying for the test, which I eventually took and did okay but not great.

After two months, I decided that bank was not the place for me, and I started my job hunt again. I was once again hired under the pretense of improving the operations, this time with my current company. Although it had a rough start, this company would be the place where I would do much of my leadership development and professional growth. This company would become more than a place of employment but also a second home where I would face so many of the same battles I was struggling with in my personal life. It was a true test of my character, abilities, and strength. My resilience would prevail, and I would encounter as many successes as obstacles.

My time with this company has been met with a unique mix of support and resistance. My boss, a white male, advocated for me and gave me the space to develop my skills, but at the same time, stifled my growth as a leader. He protected me from the constant criticism and "inappropriate" comments from his colleagues, but he also didn't allow me to confront the issues to make cultural changes, which allowed the toxic environment to ferment. It rarely felt like a safe place outside of his office where he gave me the space to say anything I needed to. He gave me a safe space where I could vacillate between the "hood" Nancy and the "corporate America" Nancy. He also gave me the space and trust to make decisions and develop new skills. Although he didn't create opportunities for me, he wasn't intimidated by me, which gave me the resources to tackle new areas of the business to run. It was a good relationship during the inception of my career, and it was so much better than what I'd experienced prior.

There were other important individuals that would impact my overall development significantly. Some of these individuals helped me grow through conflict and constantly testing my character while others mentored me. It seems as though I had one person who advocated for me over the past few years. He struggled with his own leadership while he himself grew with me. It was the perfect mix of positive and negative to create synergy. The environment lent itself to frustration, anger, and enlightenment. It is interesting that I grew at work at the same rate that I grew in my personal life. All of these relationships with men helped shape my current view of the world and myself.

I continued to advocate for others at a different level. I started to speak out with some caution at times while at others with no second thought of how it would affect me. It felt like a constant sense of responsibility to give others the kind of support I lacked. It was really scary, and I was often alone. However, the more influence I gained, the more adamant I became about helping others. The more I was exposed to in terms of the decisions behind closed doors and how those decisions were made, the more the fire inside burned towards advocacy.

As I became more aware of my strengths and abilities to lead, the stronger I felt; however, the fear would continue to exist at equal intensity. I was always afraid of being fired or making a big enough mistake that would cause havoc in my life. The pressure of being the breadwinner and of my unstable marriage would make my work situation feel more intense. It was a constant push-and-pull environment. The more I excelled at work, the more pressure I felt at home because my husband always made me feel like I wasn't good enough. It all worked together to cause complete chaos in my nervous system. My glass was starting to overflow, and no one could see it—including me.

I experienced a sense of relief through school and education. The more I learned about discrimination, bias, and the experiences of minorities in the corporate world, the more validated I felt. It also empowered me with information and the language to advocate for myself and others. School was hard though, with so many sacrifices, particularly by myself and my kids. I neglected myself first by not sleeping, eating well, or exercising—never mind the kids. I needed my husband to step up and take some of the kid load, but he didn't. Instead, I had to figure out how to juggle it all. My daughters ended up taking care of their younger siblings, while my husband focused on "helping me" with my schoolwork because he knew best. Looking back on the dynamic, I realize that it was his way of feeling superior, and I fed right into it. It's so easy to get swept into someone else's darkness. The entire experience was exhausting and, honestly, I don't know where the strength to keep going came from. I was so focused on the end game even when I had no idea what that would be.

Juggling school and work meant constantly re-prioritizing my life. It was either work and family or school and family—except that work could never be neglected since that is how I took care of all of us. It was a constant game of catch-up. I was drowning all the time. I was in a constant state of anxiety, which I processed as energy or a sense of urgency. It was only when the anxiety was overwhelming within my body that I would recognize it. It was such a struggle to parent, deal with an abusive husband, and perform at a job where I constantly felt threatened.

Yet, despite all this stress, I graduated with honors. It might sound like a great achievement—and yes, it was!—but it was also very detrimental to my body and mind. I was under so much self-imposed pressure to be great that I numbed myself to all the pain and powered through. While I am grateful for the ground I gained and what I achieved, I realize today that it could have been a very different story. I am not sure what helped me get through those lonely and painful times, but I am deeply grateful for the outcome.

Due to the life changes since my separation and the pandemic, I've had the opportunity to experience a lot of personal growth that has led me to find my most authentic self. Finally allowing myself to be authentic has opened an entirely new world of deep connections with others. In some fashion, I have developed the ability to learn from a place of curiosity. This has opened me up to others from a vulnerable place and created safety for my peers. I am not saying I show up like that one hundred percent of the time; however, when I feel safe enough, I am able to do it, which has created a wonderful new dynamic. I believe shifting my energy and my vulnerability elevated my ability to lead. I was suddenly receiving invites to speak at industry and non-industry events, be a guest on podcasts, and join groups/boards. It also strengthened my relationships with my peers within my organization. It was as if, suddenly, I attracted the positivity I was projecting.

I also credit the work I was doing at school for my doctorate, writing this book, the healing work, and feeling safe in my own body all coming together to propel me into this space of love. The love I am referring to is love for humanity at micro and macro levels. Suddenly, I saw people through their own trauma or mental health and less through how much they were a threat to me. I started to experience empathy and connection at a whole new level allowing me to lead from a place of compassion and commitment.

A few months into the pandemic, I was given the opportunity to step into the COO position, which was a surreal experience. This change created more space between myself and my fears or perceived threats. I felt safer than I had before with strong support from my boss. While our relationship continued to deepen as we learned to work together in the new largely remote environment, navigating unknown territory, he supported my growth within the industry, and more opportunities knocked on my door. The biggest career challenges I'd ever known presented themselves and I jumped at the opportunity. However, I didn't do anything alone. My team grew and became more resilient, knowledgeable, and remarkable. It continues to be an amazing ride as I am now the president of this extraordinary organization that I call my home.

**REFLECTIONS FROM RECOVERY**

- » Women and girls have to be prepared to deal with sexual harassment before entering the work place.
- » Teaching girls how to deal with sexual harassment includes giving them language to speak about it.
- » Minorities have to be prepared to deal with microaggressions as well as overt racism.
- » Advocacy work is everyone's job.
- » These trainings should be part of onboarding.
- » Therapy can help deal with work-related challenges as well as personal ones.
- » Our traumas can show up at work.
- » A toxic work environment can trigger trauma.
- » A toxic work environment can be traumatizing in itself.

## Chapter 8 - Rediscovering My True Self

My recovery, I realize, became my journey. It was difficult to recover while I continued the same patterns in my life. I had to go back to the very beginning and unpack the place in my body and mind where the initial pain resided. After months in individual therapy dealing with the abusive romantic relationships in my life, I finally paused enough to look at the deepest and most painful scar I carried. I had told Sandi about my stepfather's verbal sexual abuse and my father's abandonment, but I had barely mentioned this critical incident because it was way too much. Sandi asked me to write an account of the events of that night with as much detail as possible. Her instructions were to include smells, the temperature, lighting, colors, and any other seemingly tiny or insignificant details I could remember.

I put it off for a while since it was incredibly hard to find the time or space in my overly invasive life. Then one day, I began writing and kept writing until I was done. It was about three pages long, and in those pages, I had recalled images and memories I'd worked really hard for twenty-five years to forget. It was an interesting experience in that once I opened myself up, it all poured out. I cried a little while recalling and writing some of the details; however, I never allowed myself to fully submerge in the memory. I maintained a safe distance to allow myself the space to function when I was done. I saved it without reading it and emailed it to Sandi before too many emotions crept out. I closed my laptop and returned to my unsafe life.

At our next session, Sandi explained to me that we would go over it line by line, she would ask me questions to fill in the gaps, then I would read it when it was all finished. Before we started to actively work on it, she asked me to read it aloud, and then we explored my feelings. I explained that it was like reading a story about someone else. I could faintly see images, but I didn't feel much of anything—I didn't want to feel anything. I had buried all and any feelings I had about it so deep I could recount the event without any emotion. I could even recount watching myself laying there being raped as an out of body experience.

After I read it out loud, Sandi she asked me if I felt anything, and I asked, "no, is that bad?" She explained that my fifteen-year-old mind wasn't equipped to process such an event so I disassociated in order to survive the overwhelming fear and pain. In reality, I was deeply afraid to unbury that event. I was so scared of meeting fifteen-year-old Nancy and to know how she felt about life. I was afraid to look her in the eye and know I let her down. I felt so sorry for that girl who had been hurt by so many people. A girl who had been betrayed by many, particularly the people who were supposed to protect her.

And so it began, the true hard work that would help me embark on the true recovery I needed. The first time I told Sandi I'd been raped by my brother I didn't have the language, so I described it as my brother having sex with me. This statement was riddled with shame and guilt. I didn't understand at the time that the sheer ten-year age difference when it happened dictated the dynamics. Even though I wanted to think I was grown, I was just a child and he was an adult with a fully developed brain. I will note that the relationship between the victim and the predator alone can dictate the dynamic so there doesn't have to be an age gap because our familial relationship had as much to do with it as the age did. Other aspects that I didn't understand were the drug use and the history of domestic violence in my family, particularly his role as an abuser.

Sandi's introduction of the words rape and incest were monumental. It validated my fear, pain, lack of trust, and resentment towards everyone. I now had been given permission to use language that allowed me to stop feeling guilty and shameful. It allowed me to know that it wasn't my fault, and I didn't do anything to cause it. I did not deserve to be raped. It was not my fault.

Over the next twelve months, we would continue to work on the narrative amidst constant interruptions from my chaotic life. I would spend time on my kids, toxic marriage, and unstable work environment. Still, we worked hard to return to it month after month until we were done with what was now a ten-page extraordinarily detailed recount of the event.

The changes in the dynamic with my maternal family happened both quickly and slowly. Up to this point, I had maintained a relationship with my brother to satisfy my mother and the family status quo. The years of suppressed emotions were starting to come out in the safest way possible: through anger. It is interesting that anger often feels like the safest emotion for survivors of anything. Anger is this all-encompassing state where we can live for a long period of time to mask shame, guilt, hurt, embarrassment, resentment, and an array of other negative feelings. It comes so easily to most of us and feels so much safer than the pain that all those other feelings bring. I guess that is what I learned as a child from my caretakers. My dad used anger as his only way of expressing negative emotions, and my mother never talked to me about it or showed me how to experience other negative feelings. It's like the whole toxic masculinity thing—except it doesn't only apply to men. It applies to any of us who learn to interact with our feelings in that way.

The anger gave me an outlet, and I ran with it. I cut my brother off after all those years of pretending we were fine. It was really driven by his cruelty towards other people, but still, I finally did it. One day, I told my mother I didn't want him in my house or around my kids ever again. She, of course, insisted I was overreacting and could not understand why I suddenly wanted this change in our lives. I would say things like 'you know what he did' or 'you know why I am so angry', but she just pretended not to understand. The same thing happened with my sister as time passed.

After a while, I finally had the courage to say it out loud using the new language I had learned in therapy. I was alone with my mother in the kitchen when I said, "you know he raped me." I had to repeat it several times because it was as though I was speaking a foreign language. She was so confused and really in shock that it wasn't registering. Once she realized I wasn't changing the subject or backing down, she said, "it was both of your faults because you were drinking together." I felt exasperated, but continued to highlight all the reasons I was a victim and could not consent. I pointed out the ten-year age difference, that I was only fifteen years old, that he gave me alcohol and drugs, and that even if none of those things had been present, the mere familial relationship was enough to create a power dynamic. She couldn't hear me or even see me.

Her own pain from shame and guilt were so overwhelming that she went into defensive mode. She had to defend her narrative at all costs to protect herself from the implications of what I was telling her. The idea that her son, who she gave birth to and mostly raised, had hurt her youngest daughter was too much for her. It was inconceivable that these were her children and that her baby had been hurt this way. We had this same conversation several times over the course of a year. Each time I brought it up, I was pushier and stronger in my language. I used words like rape, incest, and betrayal. Then finally one day she said, "I asked him, and he said he is really sorry." It was both painful and validating because it meant that it actually happened. I didn't imagine it, I didn't dream it, I really lived it.

During that year, our relationship was in turmoil. My mother's voice unleashed rage within me; all twenty-five years of suppressed feelings were aimed at her. Eventually, I told her to stop coming to my house and I vowed to never return to hers since my brother lived in her second-floor apartment, and she didn't want to ask him to leave. I felt betrayed yet again. I also brought up my stepfather's verbal sexual abuse, which she completely denied. This time, I went to my sister for validation. She remembered everything, which put my mind at ease.

I stopped all interactions with my mother, sister, and brother at this point. Simultaneously, Sandi and I finished the narrative and read it from beginning to end. I lived the rape again this time, fully present, and I survived. It was one of the greatest achievements in my life, and now I had suddenly found a new strength and belief in myself. I had finally returned that guilt to its rightful owner, my brother and family. It was never mine to carry, but I did for twenty-five years. I carried the shame and guilt as though I had committed a crime. I carried it as though I had betrayed my family and did this terrible thing that created a dark cloud over us. I held the secret close to my heart because I felt I was to blame until I realized I was simply a victim and the shame was his and theirs, not mine. I look at a fifteen-year-old now and see a child, but when I looked at myself at that age, I saw an adult. I was just a child.

Suddenly, I could breathe again. The heaviest load I'd been carrying was lifted from my shoulders. My heart, mind, and body felt lighter. I could suddenly see myself again in a new light. The self-loathing and disappointment were still there, but it was as though a thick fog was becoming less dense and I could finally see my silhouette in the mirror. Looking back, I can see how overcoming that incident made me feel more worthy of love, and I started to see the toxicity around me. My home situation became clearer. It was almost as though I was stepping away from my life and watching from the outside. The same clarity started to happen at work. I realized that the path I'd abandoned years ago was calling me back. And so, the work continued—except now I was focusing on other toxic people in my life. The second major game changer for me to recognize other toxic situations at a distance. Distance between me and the toxic person helped me see the destructive patterns that kept me stuck.

The next big step was getting divorced, which can be incredibly scary. It took courage to make that leap, although I knew it was best for my children and me. The marriage and divorce were equally traumatic and damaging, yet it felt like the only option if happiness was my goal for my family. In time, I learned that my goal wasn't happiness, it was peace and calm. It took some time to make my home into a safe space. My body and mind didn't understand that we were finally safe. I did everything I could to make my home my own for the first time. I changed everything I could within the house including the paint on the walls. I started with my bedroom, which was a great source of painful memories. I wanted to reclaim my life—and so my road to full recovery began, and so did my true journey.

Over the next few months, I would spend most of my energy attempting to understand the patterns in my life. I often felt shame for continuing to engage with toxic people, toxic relationships, and enduring physical and emotional abuse. I felt responsible in the same way I felt responsible for being raped or being abused as a child. That shame kept me trapped in those relationships attempting to control the outcome by working harder and harder to gain approval and love. So, the first lesson I had to learn was self-forgiveness. I had to forgive myself for not understanding what happened, for my response, for my inability to stand up for myself, and most of all for how I treated myself during those years. For all the negative self-talk, the toxic narratives in my head, and for continuing to seek the approval of my family and the abusive men in my life. I thought I needed validation from them when I really just needed validation from myself.

While I was working through self-forgiveness, I decided that I wanted to understand my childhood wounds and trauma. It is important that we acknowledge the roles of our caretakers or family in the shaping of who we think we are. I wanted to understand why I constantly feel this pressure to be the best at everything to an unhealthy extent. The pressure that makes me feel like if I don't look a certain way or achieve constantly, I am not good enough to be loved. This is the thought process that makes me susceptible to toxic and abusive relationships. And so, I went back to the beginning again.

I looked back to my childhood, working hard to bring up the memories that were always there but that I worked really hard not to acknowledge. I thought about my childhood and how I romanticized my relationship with my dad. For years, I created a narrative that spared me the reality of who my father was. I was sure my dad adored me, and I still think he did; however, he didn't know how to love me. I had to be honest about our relationship, who he was, and his humanity. My dad was a handsome and charismatic man with amazing energy and tons of demons. He was raised by his mom, who I don't know anything about; what I do know is that he never had a father. His father was a complete stranger who didn't even acknowledge him when he saw him on the street. I don't know if his mom was emotionally available, a kind person, or even present for him. All I knew is that I desperately desired his love and attention, but he was never able to give that to me.

Once accepted the truth of who he was—an abusive husband and father, a serial cheater, a charmer, a witty and handsome man who had no self-control—everything changed. I was initially overwhelmed with rage toward him. I was angry because he was a shitty dad who caused the divorce and traumatized me. He taught me that love is conditional and that my gifts of physical beauty and intelligence were what made me worthy. He taught me love was angry and hurtful and that abandonment was imminent. It was his fault I was sexually assaulted, raped, and physically abused by several men I had romantic relationships with. I needed him to take responsibility for what he did. So, I wrote him an email in September of 2020 in which I told him all that. He never responded and even stopped communicating with me all together. The pain was deep and strong and heavy, and I sat in it day in and day out.

Then in February of 2021, I was speaking during a virtual conference, and I shared publicly for the first time that I am a survivor of sexual assault. It was a huge deal for me to say that out loud in that setting. I remember how big my emotions felt in a million different ways. I felt brave and strong but also extraordinarily vulnerable. When the talk ended and I tried to work through those feelings, I got a text. It was my dad. After months of no communication, he said I love you. I cried so hard—just like a baby. I cried like I was that scared five-year-old who needed her daddy's love and protection but whose dad was in so much of his own pain that he couldn't see her. I cried for me and for him. I cried because I knew at that moment that he did love me deeply but just didn't know how to show it. I felt his pain and shame. I knew he already knew all the things I said in my email but secretly hoped I didn't also know them. I knew his pain ran deep just like mine, and I didn't even know his story. I didn't know why he had pain. I didn't know who did or didn't love him. I didn't know about his hurt because all he knew how to show was his anger and the mask. It wasn't me who was broken, it was the entire lineage of trauma passed on from parent to child generation after generation. It wasn't lack of love, it was lack of tools and understanding.

This was an important aspect of my self-forgiveness. It allowed me to reconcile that the trauma came from others while also understanding how it was affecting me as an adult. The journey has many ups and downs because we are undoing years of trauma. It's not a linear process or even a clear process. It has many peaks and valleys filled with pain and joy. I never got a chance to tell my dad I forgave him because he died in May of 2021. However, I did get to give him and his family financial assistance during his final days and to text him that I loved him. I am confident that he understood how our pain and love intersected.

In June of 2020, I also resumed my relationships with my mom and sister. We started slow, with one meal at a local restaurant with minimal conversation and no physical contact. Over time, we met occasionally until we built up to getting together again for family celebrations full of hugs and kisses. I was finally able to see them as humans who are complicated and layered. I had to distance myself from those toxic relationships, create boundaries, and create a whole new safe place for them. I had to reset the boundaries during those years that we didn't interact. I waited until it felt safe and I felt strong enough to reinforce my boundaries as needed.

Being able to finally see my mother and sister as a humans who are flawed but good has allowed me to see myself in the same way. It takes away this rigid black-and-white mentality that created this illusion of myself in this constant negative view. How could I forgive them when I couldn't forgive myself? And how could I forgive myself when I couldn't forgive them? The lesson was that we were all in survival mode, which means we are not the best versions of ourselves. While surviving, we use any coping mechanisms available to us and often we learn those from our family—hence the generational trauma. Also, coping mechanisms are often unconscious behaviors that give us a sense of control and are born from fear. They did what they needed to in order to stay alive when they felt they were in danger. My mother learned her mechanisms when she was a child with an abusive mother and no one to protect her. My sister learned her mechanisms when my father abused her and my mother didn't have the tools to help herself or her kids. I learned my mechanisms from my parents and siblings. My children have learned from me, and so it goes on from generation to generation until someone has the tools to understand the harmful effects and change the behaviors.

Forgiving myself has allowed me a space to accept and love myself. Learning to accept and love myself was harder than all of the other work I'd done up to this point. I had to accept that I made decisions based on what I knew at the time and what I felt. I didn't understand that violence felt familiar to my body although my logical brain knew it was bad. I didn't realize that red flags were a familiar place that felt like my childhood and created a false sense of control. I didn't know that my body's response of fear and anxiety to abusive men felt like excitement and attraction because I never learned the difference. How could I seek out safe love in a partner when I didn't love myself and I didn't know what safe love looked like? We can't understand what we don't know, and we won't know until we take the time to learn.

I remember asking Sandi once why I suddenly cared about all these things and wanted to dive into my trauma. She explained that I had reached a point where I felt my basic needs were met and was paying attention to my feelings for the first time. Six years ago when I started seeing Sandi, I had reached a point in my career that provided financial stability and security. I was finally able to support my family in a way that didn't feel like we would be in a shelter next month. I finally felt like I was stable—not wealthy but stable. I had spent so much time in my life in poverty and instability that survival meant being able to pay rent and buy food at the same time. It meant that my kids had stability and even some comforts although I didn't have the safety part figured out. I needed help with the safety part because that was so deeply ingrained in me that I couldn't get out on my own.

Over the next few months, I experienced enormous growth with many challenges and falls in between. The growth came through occasional moments of deep insight or big moments of strong scary feelings or even a kind gesture by one of the many people who cared for me. Our family went through a deep transformation as we were all on the same journey together while also walking on our own paths. I was finally able to give my children the love and acceptance they deserved since I was finally able to do the same for myself. How could they love themselves unconditionally when I taught them every day that I didn't do the same? How could I model something I didn't know or understand? Loving myself allowed me to show them true, unconditional love.

Of course, this didn't come easily overnight. It is a conscious decision we must make every day. I had to see the negative narratives the five-year-old who lives inside me was creating to protect me. For years I couldn't even consciously hear the negative narrative playing over and over in my head. I had to dive deep into my feelings both good and bad. It took many scary moments and vulnerable conversations to get there. I learned what a trigger was and how to detect it. I acknowledged that I lived in a constant state of hyper vigilance and anxiety. I had to spend time alone with my real thoughts and feelings. I had to teach myself to quiet down the childhood fears screaming in my head so I could listen to my adult needs.

I learned that I want to continue to learn and evolve, but that it can't happen until I find my true self, which was uncomfortable to say the least. I honestly didn't know who I was or what I even really liked. I'd spent so much time being who I thought I needed to be to be loved that I had no idea who my authentic self was. I played a part at work to fit in and be given an opportunity to succeed in a highly caucasian, male, and elitist environment. I had to play a part in the abusive relationships with the men in my life. I played a role within my dysfunctional family dynamics. And finally, I played a role with my children that was mostly a result of unconscious behaviors that were toxic. Who the hell was the real me in all these roles that I played to survive in unsafe environments.

As I was learning to spend time alone when my younger kids went away for a week at a time and my older kids were now adults, Sandi asked me I liked to do. I genuinely didn't know how to answer. I began to question everything I did. I questioned all my relationships, how I reacted to almost everything and everyone. I started to wonder how much of what I did every day was authentic. It was complicated because I now knew how often I did things to seek approval, and how often my abusive partners used my insecurities against me. I recall being told I couldn't write a sentence and that I was "ghetto" by a partner. I remember having my body and appearance judged harshly by that same partner and being rejected for gaining weight. I was told I was a bad mother repeatedly and that my friends only pretended to like me to advance their careers. Each of those comments hurt me and chipped away at me along with all the violence that plagued my home. I heard how unworthy of love I was for years and years, so now I had to shake off that narrative, along with the ones from my childhood, to find myself; I had to get cut out all those voices to find my own.

I started small by doing the things I had done since I was a kid like going to the beach. The beach had been my favorite place in the world since I could remember. I loved the feeling of warmth of the sun on my skin, sand between my toes, and water against my body. The beach was a place where I felt present in my body. I also rediscovered how much I love to dance. I had stopped dancing for years and now my body had found the joy I had as a little girl when I moved to a good rhythm.

It took work and I knew that there was much more to it. I was also fortunate enough to be given a professional coach. She was fantastic and knew me from day one. It was that feeling of someone really seeing you. She understood me in a way that only another person who identified with me could. As a woman of color and a professional, she got my struggles, and for the first time I felt as though I was truly seen. She sent me this book The Universe Has Your Back by Gabrielle Bernstein, and damn that book opened me up to all new possibilities for growth and hope.

Almost simultaneously, my boss sent me the book What happened to You by Oprah and Dr. Perry. This book opened me up to a new level of understanding the effects of trauma and the body. It helped me understand my physical responses to stress in a new way. I was just starting to learn the difference between anxiety, stress, and good energy. I noticed my heart rate increasing when I received a triggering email from a toxic ex-partner or when my colleagues triggered me at work. I had all these new resources and tools that I could either reject because of the vulnerability they presented, or I could embrace them. My coach doubled down on what Sandi said, however, she put it into work context which was also full of toxicity in some respects. I began read everything I could about generational trauma, recovering from abusive romantic relationships, and how trauma manifested in our behaviors.

All this brought me to a place where I had to own my journey. I could continue to focus on how I got here, who hurt me how and when, or I could own it. I could take control of how my coping mechanisms played out in my romantic relationships as well as within my family. I started to pay attention to how I spoke to my kids and how I interacted with potential partners, who I was attracted to, why, and most all of how my body felt around those people. I started to pay attention to how my children trigged my shame and guilt, and in turn how I responded to them. It was all interrelated, but it all started with self-love. I named my ego so I could separate from that scared inner child and comfort her. I created a safe space in my home with boundaries for myself and my kids. It is a work in progress every day; however, it is always in the forefront of my mind.

Once I started to open myself up to the journey and focused on my purpose I opened up to new possibilities. I chose vulnerability over protecting my ego and my heart. I decided that I would share my authentic self with the world one act at a time. I became vulnerable with my children in a whole new way. I openly shared what I was learning about my past and present. I started by learning to apologize to them and by honoring them in the way I wasn't honored. I worked towards conscientious parenting, which is harder than the alternative. I started to model self-love, self-care, and self-acceptance for them. I provided a space for them to continue to grow within so they wouldn't have to choose between their family and their peace. Once I stopped judging myself and started using kind words towards myself, I stopped judging them and had more kindness for them.

The changes in our home have been gradual and even subtle in some ways but impactful. All the kids are still struggling as they recover from years of a toxic household, but they are all thriving in their own way. We openly talk about generational trauma, abuse, coping mechanisms, and therapy. We participated in BLM protests in 2020 and were heavily involved in politics as we channeled our pain in a positive way. We have since moved towards community, individual causes, and staying mindful of our emotional capacity. We have learned to connect on a more personal and genuine level without the need to share all opinions. We are all becoming more authentic and figuring out what we each like. We are finally free to be ourselves without fear.

It takes work for me to give up forty-eight years of unconscious behavior based on years of doing my best to survive. I catch myself making mistakes all the time. The difference now is that I try to be kind to myself instead of shaming myself. The biggest difference is that when I shame myself, I feel guilty and embarrassed and respond from a defensive place. Apologizing with a true effort to be better feels like the best strategy in a parent-child relationship, just like any other. How can we love our kids so much but not be willing to apologize when it is obvious that we messed up? We often save compassion, kindness, and empathy for the outside world and don't save any for ourselves or our children. We must start with us to have room for everyone else.

While all this learning and unlearning was going on at home, my career has been thriving more than ever. An opportunity for an interview presented itsel,f and I jumped on it. It was an opportunity to do the work beyond my home for my community. It was another opportunity to be authentic and continue to work towards my passion and purpose, to use my story to have a positive impact on others. Suddenly, many opportunities presented themselves, one after the other, and I was open to each and every one. I was learning to trust in the journey and give up the need for total control. I started to understand that my need for control was born from a place of survival.

During my journey, I have discovered how deep my connections are with my old and new friends. I have continued to learn to listen to my body when it senses toxicity. I am learning to ground myself when I am triggered and use my resources instead of returning to my old coping mechanisms. I struggle all the time while striving to improve. I have learned to use kind words when I speak to myself and recognize when the negative thoughts try to creep in. I hug myself in the shower when I cry, which happens often. I cry for the child version of me who still feels afraid at times. I cry for the lost years, the lost dreams, and disappointment. I continue to forgive myself for the past, for the many times my children were hurt by the toxic men in my life, and most of all I am kind to myself.

I remind myself that I am worthy of love. I choose to love others and reject hatred, anger, and negativity. I embrace my gift, the ability to love others and see beyond the pain. Embrace your gift, love freely, and start by loving yourself deeply.

## REFLECTIONS FROM RECOVERY

- » Recovery is hard.
- » Recovery includes mental and physical health.
- » Therapy is not usually enough.
- » Self care isn't spas and masks.
- » Self care is time alone, finding our inner child and feeling the pain.
- » We must feel our feelings to get past them.
- » Crying is good for the soul.
- » I learned to hug myself in a way that felt satisfying.
- » We absolutely can't fully love anyone (kids, partner, friends) until we love ourselves.
- » Finding what makes you connect with yourself and your intuition is everything.
- » I found the Universe.

## RECOMMENDED RESOURCES AND INFORMATION

- » ACES quiz
  https://americanspcc.org/take-the-aces-quiz/
- » Maslow's Hierarchy of needs helps to illustrate why safety and survival come first
- » *What Happened to You* by Oprah Winfrey and Dr. Bruce D. Perry
- » *The Universe Has Your Back* by Gabrielle Bernstein

## About the Author

Nancy was born in Costa Rica in 1973 and moved to America in 1981 with her sister and mother where they experienced poverty, food insecurity, and violence at every turn. As the first high school graduate in her family, she had no guidance for exploring higher education. She worked tirelessly to obtain her A.S. in Paralegal Studies from Berkeley College while raising three kids under the age of five.

Berkeley College sent her on her first interview in the equipment finance industry in 2000. She began in an entry-level position at Fleet Capital Healthcare as a documentation processor. Then, returned to school full-time and received her B.A. in Management while also working full-time and as a single parent. In 2005, she started at Eastern Funding LLC as a mid-level documentation specialist. During her seventeen years at Eastern Funding, she received her MBA, was promoted five times, and had two more children.

During her initial seven years in therapy, she was able to start the journey to recovery. She worked on healing from generational trauma; childhood trauma; physical, emotional, and sexual abuse; and unhealthy patterns of self-abandonment to toxic partners.

Today, she has worked her way up to President of her company and speaks nationally on human issues in the workplace such as DEI, leadership, mental health, and company culture. She serves on several boards advocating for these causes and engages in advocacy work through other avenues. She is focusing on loving herself and modeling self-love for her children, grandchildren, and communities.

www.ingramcontent.com/pod-product-compliance
Lightning Source LLC
LaVergne TN
LVHW041533070526
838199LV00046B/1643